SCAM-FREE LIVING

HOW TO PREVENT SCAMMERS FROM STEALING YOUR HARD-EARNED MONEY

RODERICK J. SPURGEON

Copyright © 2025 Roderick J. Spurgeon

All Rights Reserved.

No part of this book may be reproduced or transmitted in any manner without the prior written consent of the publisher.

A Tioran Publishing release.

http://www.ownyourdefense.net

TABLE OF CONTENTS

	Preface	iv
	Introduction	vi
Chapter 1.	Identity theft	1
Chapter 2.	Social media	6
Chapter 3.	Passwords	11
Chapter 4.	Free Wi-Fi	18
Chapter 5.	Email scams	22
Chapter 6.	Cloud storage	39
Chapter 7.	Virus protection	45
Chapter 8.	Malware and protecting data	50
Chapter 9.	Mail theft	55
Chapter 10.	Document shredding	60
Chapter 11.	Telephone scams	64
Chapter 12.	Foreign lottery scams	72
Chapter 13.	Classified ad scams	78
Chapter 14.	Work from home scams	85
Chapter 15.	Door-to-door scams	92
Chapter 16.	Internet dating scams	99
Chapter 17.	Shop smart	103
Chapter 18.	Investment scams	111
Chapter 19.	Charitable donations	116
Chapter 20.	Friends and family	121
Chapter 21.	Monitor your credit	130
Chapter 22.	How to spot a thief	136
Chapter 23.	How to get rid of a telescammer	140
Chapter 24.	If you've been scammed	143
Chapter 25.	Helpful websites	146
Chapter 26.	About Own Your Defense	148

PREFACE

Imagine being fooled by a criminal into giving away your money. It would feel like a gut-wrenching punch to the stomach—a mix of loss, betrayal, and helplessness. This is the reality for thousands of people around the world every day, as scammers and thieves prey on the trusting nature of individuals.

To protect yourself from these criminals, there's only one solution: spot their scams on sight and shut them down immediately. However, recognizing a scam isn't as straightforward as you might think. Some criminals are exceptionally clever, adept at slipping past your initial skepticism.

Fraud recognition and avoidance are crucial life skills. You might wonder if it's really worth your time, given the sheer number of people in the world. But if you have a cell phone, an email address, or a place you call home, you can be targeted. Criminals can and will find you, aiming to steal what's rightfully yours.

It might not happen today or tomorrow, but without proper defenses, a criminal will eventually breach your barriers and access what you hold dear. The best way to prepare is by staying informed and maintaining your knowledge. Learn about the latest scams and techniques to protect yourself. Read blogs, government websites, books, and watch videos on scams. Arm yourself with the knowledge needed to keep yourself and your loved ones safe.

You don't need to spend countless hours each day preparing for an attack. Just set aside an hour or two each month to learn something new about scams. Visit different websites, read diverse books, or watch varied videos. The key is to build your knowledge over time. As you gain wisdom, your chances of falling victim to a scam will decrease.

I believe one of the best ways to learn is through stories. Stories are easier to remember and more engaging than dry, rigid content. In this book, I've applied that philosophy to teach you how to avoid becoming a scammer's next victim.

Throughout Scam-Free Living, each chapter begins with a thought-provoking story, followed by practical tips to avoid the problems faced within them. These stories are fictitious, but the threats they convey are real. Embrace the knowledge shared in each story, and you'll enhance your understanding of how criminals operate and how to protect yourself from their schemes.

INTRODUCTION

"It's time to go, Mom." Gary placed a supportive hand on his mother's shoulder and opened the passenger door of his metallic green mini-van.

June smiled at her son, placing a slightly trembling hand on top of his. She took one last look at her home of 42 years, lost in a flood of warm memories. She had moved into the two-story, 2,800-square-foot home with Ward during their 10-year anniversary month. They saved every dollar they could spare to afford a good home where they could start their family. A year after they moved in, Gary was born, followed a few years later by their twin daughters, Catherine and Jenny.

The house had always been filled with love, through good times and bad. June and Ward watched their children grow into exceptional adults and start families of their own. They provided comfort and shelter to Jenny when she separated from her husband and hosted Catherine's wedding reception when she found her soul mate. Even after Ward passed away two years ago from cancer, the house still offered June a measure of peace, serving as a reminder of the wonderful life she had enjoyed with him.

June slid onto the soft leather seat of the mini-van, devastated that the house filled with so many wonderful memories couldn't be passed down to her children as she and Ward had hoped. Don, the Canadian lottery official, had been so convincing over the phone, offering June the opportunity to provide a life free from financial worry for her kids when she finally received her $2.4 million in lottery winnings. The dream of leaving her children a prosperous legacy quickly crumbled the day she received an eviction notice ordering her to vacate her home within 30 days.

She sent Don every dollar she could spare to pay insurance and processing fees on the lottery winnings, but it wasn't enough. Taxes had to be paid on the winnings before she could receive her lump sum payment, and June didn't have enough money left in savings to make the payment. That's when Don offered her an easy solution: take out a mortgage on her home to pay the taxes and pay off the loan when she received her winnings. The solution made sense to June, and Don helpfully walked her through every step in the process, including how to send such a large payment to the lottery commission.

Two months after June sent the cashier's check to Don, she still hadn't received her winnings. She called the nice, young man on many occasions during this time and was always reassured that the money was on its way. After the fourth month, when June received a foreclosure notice from her bank, she called Don again to ask when she could expect her money. That's when she found out that Don's telephone number had been disconnected. Her heart sank at the crushing discovery, and at that moment, she realized she had been victimized by a scam artist.

June picked up the phone many times afterward to call her children and ask for help, but she was embarrassed by her decision to send her money to Don. She didn't want her kids to think she was unable to care for herself and feared losing her independence if they placed her in an elder care facility. June hid her situation from her family until she received the eviction notice. With the deadline of her eviction rapidly approaching, she finally picked up the phone to ask for help.

Gary closed the mini-van door and looked at his mother sitting forlornly next to him. He did his best to save her home from foreclosure by negotiating with the bank, but the home had already been sold at auction. He tried to pool enough money with his sisters to buy the home, but the new owner wasn't interested in selling it. There was only one solution left that made sense, and Gary wasn't taking "no" for an answer.

The van's engine roared to life when Gary turned the key and backed slowly out of the driveway.

"Don't worry, Mom. Everything will be okay," Gary said reassuringly. "Karen and I have already set up the spare bedroom for you, and the kids are looking forward to spending more time with their Nana."

June gave a barely perceptible nod and wiped away a tear as she watched her home fade away in the side-view mirror.

SCAM-FREE LIVING: HOW TO PREVENT SCAMMERS FROM STEALING YOUR HARD-EARNED MONEY

Have you been scammed?

Criminals take advantage of the good, trusting nature of others to get what they want. It doesn't matter if you're rich or poor, old or young. If a criminal thinks they can take what's yours, they will try, repeatedly, to take it.

Consider yourself lucky if you have yet to be targeted by scammers, but sooner or later, they will find you.

You've worked hard for your money. You spend it wisely, shop smartly, and put some aside to enjoy a comfortable retirement. Then someone comes along and does everything possible to take it away from you.

Scam artists are everywhere, and they make their living by stealing from others. Scammers don't care about you or how you're going to survive if they take away your hard-earned money. They care about tricking you into giving them every dime you have to enrich their own lives. It's a game to them, and they intend to win. It's a game you can't afford to lose.

Preparation is often the key to winning any battle, including the one against thieves. Make no mistake, when a scammer shows up at your door, your email inbox, through your phone, or in your mailbox, you are under attack. A scammer will never announce their arrival. These scoundrels will put on friendly masks to disguise their hideous intentions and smile brightly as they raid your pockets. They will attempt to gain your trust, convince you why you should send them money, and leave you with nothing but empty promises. Scammers use words to steal, and they're masters of their craft. It's vital that you learn their tricks and prepare for attack, because sooner or later, one of these morally bankrupt people might target you. Will you be able to defend yourself if that happens?

Within the pages of this book, you'll find scammers' battle plans to wage war against you. While they may change their tactics and take advantage of new technology to implement their creative scams, there's always one consistent element in all their attacks—they want what you have. Don't give it to them.

x

CHAPTER 1

IDENTITY THEFT

"Hello?" Linda asked after opening her front door. A cool breeze brushed across her face from the gentle wind of an approaching afternoon storm.

A man in blue jeans and a tan, long-sleeved work shirt smiled back at her. "Hi. Is this..." he glanced at a clipboard and recited Linda's address.

Linda nodded. "Yes, it is."

"Good afternoon, ma'am. My name is Hank from the utility company. How are you doing today?"

"Oh, just fine," Linda said. "How are you?"

Hank peered at the sky over his shoulder. "I'll be just fine too if I can finish my rounds before the storm hits." He winked.

Linda smiled. "How can I help you?"

"Well, we're verifying account information for our customers today to make sure what we have is accurate. There have been a lot of computer break-ins, and we just want to ensure nobody has changed your information on us. We certainly wouldn't want someone pretending to be you to access your account, would we?" He flashed a disarming smile.

Linda shook her head. "No, I wouldn't want that. What do you need to know?"

"Since we already have your home address, we can skip that part. Wasn't that easy?"

Linda nodded.

"Okay, next question," Hank continued. "What's your current phone number?"

Linda gave Hank her cell phone number.

Hank scribbled on his clipboard. "Yep, that looks right. How about your date of birth? I'd say 1975 perhaps? Maybe 1974?"

Linda blushed. "It's actually July 8, 1951."

"What? No way. Are you sure that's right?"

Linda nodded shyly. "It's been the same ever since I was born."

Hank whistled in surprise. "Well, you don't look it. What's your secret to looking so young?"

Linda shrugged. "Oh, I don't know. I take vitamins every morning."

"Whatever it is, keep doing it. It's working. How about your social security number?"

Linda pushed a lock of gray hair behind her ear and recited the requested numbers.

"Looks good," Hank confirmed. "Almost done, I promise. I just need your mother's maiden name and you're all set."

After Linda gave Hank the information, he pressed a button on the end of his pen and slid the instrument into his shirt pocket.

"Well, thank you again for your help today. Say, do you mind if I give you a call sometime? You are single, right?"

"Oh, I don't know," Linda replied with barely contained interest. "Don't you think I'm a little too old for you?"

Hank made a dismissive gesture. "I always say age is only in the mind. We don't know how long we'll be on this planet, so we might as well have fun while we're here. Right?"

Linda nodded. "I guess that would be okay."

"Great! Thanks again for your help today. See you soon."

As Hank moved down the sidewalk, a crack of thunder rattled the ground underneath Linda. She closed the door and leaned against it for support. It had been some time since a younger man had shown an interest in her, and she was looking forward to Hank's call.

The only call she would receive regarding Hank would be from creditors seeking payment on numerous accounts he opened in her name.

DON'T LET SOMEONE BECOME YOU

Do you know who you are? Can you prove it to others? Identity thieves certainly can, and if they gain your personal information, they can become you.

Personal information such as your birth date, social security number, and mother's maiden name are the passcodes to your life. If this information falls into the wrong hands, a criminal can use it to steal your identity. Treat this information as you would a very personal and private secret. Give it to the wrong person, and it will cost you dearly.

If someone shows up at your doorstep, as in the story above, or calls you on the telephone claiming to be from your bank, mortgage, cable, telephone, or utility company and asks for personal information to verify your identity, you are probably in contact with an identity thief.

In this story, Hank already had Linda's name and address from the county assessor's office, but he needed much more information than that to steal her identity. Once he had what he needed, he opened new credit accounts in her name and racked up a considerable amount of debt.

Companies you do business with won't contact you to ask for your personal information. If they call you on the phone and you answer, that's all the verification they need to know it's you on the other end. Ironically, some scammers will contact you to warn that someone may have compromised one or more of your accounts. They will instill fear within you by telling you that your account is under attack and convince you that they will help protect you from harm. They have become your savior, and they'll use your newly-forged trust in them to get every scrap of information from you that they need to steal your identity.

If you want to confirm the person on the other end of the phone is who they say they are, tell them that you'd like to verify their identity by calling the company directly. If they attempt to persuade you not to call the company, it could be a scam. If they become angry and threaten you in any way because you doubt their identity, it's almost certainly a scam. Hang up immediately and call the company to report what happened. If they give you a telephone number to call for identity verification, don't use it. It could be the scammer's phone number. Instead, call the telephone number you have on file for the company. If you don't have it handy, review an old statement to find the phone number or go to the company website and obtain the phone number from there.

Pro tip: Prepare a contact list of companies you do business with and write down the telephone and address information for them. Keep that piece of paper handy near a telephone so you can reference it quickly. You can also keep the information in your smartphone, but make sure the phone requires a passkey to gain access.

When thieves gain access to someone's personal information, they will use it to apply for credit cards, personal loans, and if they're skilled and bold enough, perhaps even a driver's license in the victim's name. They could seek employment, take out a mortgage or car loan, and even commit crimes in another person's name. The evil deeds they do may destroy an innocent person's life and could even land the victim in jail until they can prove an identity thief committed the crime. It might take years to repair the damage from some of the more serious incidents of identity theft, but even if a person fully recovers, their personal information may still exist elsewhere, such as in the dark web, and be used by other thieves.

The best way to avoid dealing with the problem is to prevent it from occurring in the first place. Remember, companies you do business with will never call you to ask for your personal information. They won't send a representative to your door to ask for your account number, telephone number, or mother's maiden name. They won't send an email asking for your social security number. They won't send a letter in the mail asking you to verify your birth date. Thieves, however, will ask for this information, and they need it to assume your identity. Don't let someone else become you.

Never respond to unsolicited requests for your personal information. If you want to verify the legitimacy of a request, call the company directly using the information on your contact list. If you haven't already done so, prepare that contact list now.

CHAPTER 2

SOCIAL MEDIA

Martha zipped the side pocket of her green, floral-patterned suitcase and rolled it next to the front door. She hadn't seen her son Michael since her birthday party four months ago, and she was looking forward to her trip to Seattle to see him.

She pressed a switch on the wall and turned off the white LED lights built into the Christmas tree. Martha debated whether to go through the hassle of setting it up this year, since she and her husband planned to spend two weeks with her son during the holidays, but she didn't want to break with tradition.

"All set?" Jim asked.

Martha nodded at her husband of 46 years. They met in college, and though he had lost most of the hair on top of his head and gained more than a few pounds since that time, her love for him had only grown stronger since the first night she felt his lips press against hers.

"Alright, I'll pull the car out of the garage." Jim pointed to Martha's case. "Leave that here. I'll take care of it when I get back."

"Oh, Jim, I can take care of my own bag. Besides, your doctor said you need to rest your back. It's only been three months since your surgery, and you need to heal."

"The day I can't carry my wife's bag for her is the day I'm beyond healing. I may have missed visiting Michael during Thanksgiving because of my back, but I'll be damned if I'm going to let it keep me from taking care of you."

Martha shook her head. "Go get the car. I'll let Michael know we're heading to the airport." She loved Jim for his persistence in caring for her, but she knew his stubbornness might someday cause more harm than good.

When Jim left the room, Martha pulled out a small tablet PC from her purse. She punched in the four-digit code to unlock it and accessed her social media account.

"Leaving for the airport in 5 minutes," she wrote in a message on Michael's social media page. "We're looking forward to spending the next two weeks with you. I'll let you know when we land. We love you!"

Martha shut down her tablet and returned it to her purse.

"We'd better get going," Jim said. "We don't want to miss the flight."

Martha hadn't heard Jim enter through the front door, but his skill at stealthy movements, honed during his time in the military, were as sharp as ever. She scowled somewhat playfully at him when he picked up her bag and stepped outside.

As the couple pulled out of their driveway and headed toward the airport, a thief monitoring potential targets on social media spotted Martha's post. He smiled at the chance to raid an unoccupied home without the possibility of interference. With a few clicks of his mouse, the thief cross-referenced her name with the county assessor's office database and identified her address.

The thief picked up his phone and dialed a number. "Bill, clear your schedule. We've got another job to do."

DON'T GIVE SCAMMERS THE KEYS TO YOUR IDENTITY THROUGH SOCIAL MEDIA

Social media accounts continue to grow in popularity with each passing year. As more people join the revolution and share their lives with others online, scammers are joining the party and learning everything they can about people who share more than they should, just as in the scenario above.

Many modern-day scammers have turned to social media to look for people who openly post such things as when they'll be taking trips out of town, which financial institutions they frequent, where they used to live when growing up, how much they miss their pets from when they were young, how much they miss their grandmothers, or where an upcoming high school reunion is located. If you post this information online and a scammer gets hold of it, it can be used by the thief to raid your home when you're not there, to assume your identity over the phone with a financial institution, or to reset passwords that secure your bank, email, social media, and other internet-based accounts.

When you create a new account at a business, you may be required to establish challenge questions to complete the setup process. These questions are designed to verify your identity to prevent unauthorized access to your accounts and to reset passwords if you forget them. Some questions ask for the street you used to live on, the name of your first pet, your mother's maiden name, or the name of your high school mascot. When you share this information on your social media account, you may also be sharing it with someone who wants to assume your identity.

Even if you only share personal information with people on your "friends" list, you risk sharing it with criminals when your friends share your information on their own page. Have you vetted all your friends' friends lists? How about their friends? You don't control where your information goes or who has access to it when it's on the internet.

Pro tip: Unless what you post on social media is something you'd share with anyone in the world, don't post it. You never know what will happen to it once it's out there.

No matter how careful you are at selecting your friends online, your friends may not be so careful in selecting theirs. A post you share can end up in the hands of someone who is anything but your friend.

If you have several social media accounts, avoid posting personal information about yourself in any of them. Criminals who target you will look for every scrap of information they can find about you, and they'll follow you through every social media account you have online to do it. Some thieves are extremely determined and will take the time to piece together the information received from each account you have to create a working profile about you. They can then use cross-referenced information to answer identity verification questions and gain control of your email, bank, and social media accounts. Once that happens, they could steal money from your checking or savings accounts, go on a shopping spree with your stolen credit card information, or use your personal information to steal your identity and cause far more severe damage.

In addition to giving careful consideration to what you post online, be sure to avoid sharing personal information with third-party social media applications that request it. This includes games, funny avatar-creation apps, match your personality or appearance with celebrity apps, IQ tests, and others. Do you know what these applications do with your information? Have you read every word of each privacy statement that explains how they can and will use the information you provide or who they can share it with?

Surprisingly, many people freely provide personal information to vendors in exchange for access to interesting software without knowing how their information will be used. Don't let an interesting or fun-looking application dupe you into giving up personal information that can be used against you later. Once you provide your personal information, you can't control who has access to it.

Anything you share on social media has the potential to go beyond whom you intend to see it. Whether it's posting your place of birth, a photo of you standing next to your new car, or a video of your family at a birthday party in your home, that item is now on the internet forever and can be used by others to determine if you're worth becoming their next victim. Even if you delete the item after you post it, some people may have already copied it to their own computers, and it may also remain on the social media computer system you posted it to indefinitely.

Remember, you don't control who has access to your information once you place it on the internet, so err on the side of caution and limit what you share online. This includes your email address, telephone number, and physical address. Criminals can use this information to pitch their scams directly to you, use it for account verification purposes, or gain access to your home when you're not around.

CHAPTER 3

PASSWORDS

Ray peered at the single-story yellow house and swallowed nervously. "Are you sure it's safe, man? The dude just left."

Charlie picked up a large, tan satchel embroidered with a "Steven's Best Contracting" logo on its side and closed the sliding van door. "It's fine. He'll be at breakfast with his old war buddies for the next two hours. Trust me. He'll never suspect a thing until we're long gone."

Ray rubbed his stubbly chin. "If you say so."

The pair of career criminals approached the home and easily picked the front door lock. Once they entered the house, Ray whistled.

"Damn, check out the T.V."

"Forget it," Charlie said. "I think his neighbors would notice if we walked out with a flat panel. Just grab whatever you can fit in your bag and let's go."

Ray nodded. "I'll check the bedroom."

When Ray left the foyer, Charlie stepped into the study and admired the hickory bookcases and matching furniture. He traced his fingers along the flat, smooth surface of the desk as he circled around it and moved toward a black leather high-back chair.

"This is the life," Charlie sighed as he flopped into the comfortable, overstuffed seat. He swiveled in the chair slowly, admiring the collection of statuettes, ornate picture frames, and an autographed football helmet amidst a large collection of books on the shelves surrounding him. He opened the central desk drawer and rummaged through a collection of papers, pens, and other odds and ends. Disappointed, Charlie turned to the pair of drawers on either side of the desk and found a letter opener in the shape of a sword, a small box containing a collection of cigars, and a mostly full bottle of brandy among a collection of paperwork. He tucked the useful items into his duffel and turned his attention to the surface of the desk.

Charlie's eyes focused on an old, Civil War-style cannon. He picked it up and pressed down on a thumb trigger at its rear. When he did, a bright blue flame erupted from its mouth. With an amused smile, Charlie stowed the item in his duffel. He turned his attention to a 24" monitor on the corner of the desk, which displayed an interesting pattern of multi-colored lines streaking across its screen.

"Marcy's been wanting a new one of these," Charlie muttered aloud. He moved to disconnect the monitor when he spotted a yellow sticky note on the desk in front of it. On the note, he saw a collection of websites, usernames, and passwords scrawled in neat handwriting. A broad smile spread across Charlie's face.

"Score!" he said in celebration. Charlie grabbed the note and quickly stuffed it into his right pants pocket. He picked up the duffel from the floor and was about to leave the room when he remembered the monitor. With a few flicks of his wrist, Charlie unplugged the high-definition, lightweight object, hefted it up from the desk, and placed it carefully into his bag.

When Charlie returned to the foyer, Ray joined him from the bedroom.

"All I found were a few pieces of cheap jewelry, an old revolver from before the Stone Age, and $123," Ray said dejectedly. "What a tightwad."

"You know they didn't have revolvers in the Stone Age, right?" Charlie corrected.

Ray shrugged. "I don't know. I wasn't there."

Charlie shook his head. "Whatever. Forget what you found. I just picked up the virtual keys to his cash. Come on. We've got some shopping to do."

PASSWORDS ARE YOUR DIGITAL SECURITY GUARDS. MAKE THEM STRONG.

A key to your personal vehicle is something only you have access to, unless you share it with others. A password is like a key for your car.

A good password has different characteristics such as numbers, letters, and symbols to give your digital accounts a higher level of protection, just as a key has grooves and/or a microchip to gain access to your car. You keep the keys to your car safe to prevent unauthorized people from having their way with your property, and the same should also be true for your passwords.

While most people have passwords for one or more internet-based accounts and personal devices, not all passwords are good ones. Think of a bad password as a poorly crafted key. If the key to your car was shaped like a nail file, anyone with a nail file could take your car if they wanted to do so. The same is true for bad passwords. If your passwords are simple and easy to guess, hackers can gain access to your accounts and do whatever they like with them.

Here are some password sources you should never use to secure your accounts:

- The name of a family member, friend, or pet

- A familiar birth date, Social Security number, address, or phone number

- Your favorite anything, such as a novel, car, movie, food, or clothing brand

- Any combination of the above

The best passwords include words not connected to you. One way to develop this type of password is to open a dictionary and randomly point to a word. Flip to another page and identify another word. Mix pieces of the two words together and add a few numbers and symbols to the mix. Include at least one uppercase letter, one number, and one symbol. Here are a few examples of stronger passwords, but don't use them! Create your own so people who read this can't figure out what they are.

- delT49!bu&

- CrSH7PRTO^$

- HAwire*dra?8

These are complex passwords and might be hard for you to remember, especially if you have many accounts. While the goal of a password is to secure your account from access by others, it shouldn't prevent you from accessing your own account. What would be the point of creating digital accounts only to block your own access to them?

One way to keep your passwords handy is to write them down on a piece of paper and place it where others aren't likely to look. As you read in the scenario above, placing passwords in a location convenient to you might also make them accessible to others. If you want to store passwords on a piece of paper to keep them handy, there are far better options than placing them near your computer.

Place the password list inside a book on your bookshelf (if you have a large collection of books), inside the back of a picture frame (if you have many picture frames), or a locked safe to secure your password list. A safe is probably your best bet for its increased security, but the other locations should work as an alternative if you don't have one. Also, don't identify the passwords as passwords or the accounts they belong to on that piece of paper, just in case someone finds it. You might consider adding other words or phrases to the paper to make it appear as gibberish should it fall into the wrong hands.

Another option to consider for keeping passwords safe is to store them in a password-protected word processing document on your computer. You only have to remember a single password for the document to have access to all your other passwords. Be sure to also add a password for your computer. Yes, it's another password to remember, but it's also an additional layer of protection against criminals.

An alternative to storing the password file on your computer, or perhaps in addition to it, just in case it malfunctions, would be to store the list of passwords on an encrypted flash drive. Encrypted flash drives are inexpensive, depending on the type and storage capacity selected, and you can set a single password to keep all the contents safe. Type "encrypted flash drive" in your favorite search engine to locate one for sale. I'd recommend selecting one with the highest reviews rather than the lowest price. You don't know how a device will serve your needs, so choosing one that worked successfully for others is the next best thing.

If you place the list of passwords exclusively on a flash drive, be sure to keep it in a memorable location to avoid losing access to your accounts. As mentioned above, the best location to keep passwords is inside a safe, but if you don't have one, try storing it in a location a thief wouldn't think of looking, such as inside your home network cabinet, inside the battery compartment of an old, beat-up flashlight, or inside an empty container of sour cream in your refrigerator.

When creating passwords for your online accounts, each account should have its own separate password. If all your accounts have the same password, and someone manages to guess what it is, that person will have access to all your accounts. Creating a separate password for each of your accounts will also come in handy if you feel compelled to lend someone access to your video streaming, audio streaming, gaming, or other entertainment account but don't want that person to access any other account you have. It might be a pain to maintain so many separate passwords, especially if you have a lot of them, but the pain will be far worse if the wrong person gets hold of your information and exploits it. Better separate than sorry.

As an additional measure of precaution, change your passwords periodically, such as every six months or once per year. If a hacker gains access to one or more of your passwords, you may not know about the intrusion for some time. Hackers may siphon information from your account over time, making sure not to leave any tell-tale signs that they accessed it. They might amass a treasure trove of data on you, your accounts, and anything else they have access to in a compromised account. By changing your passwords periodically, you prevent long-term access to your accounts by a stealthy intruder.

If you ever find out that someone discovered your password

and gained access to one of your accounts, change the passwords for all your accounts. The thief may have gained access to more than one of your passwords, and you need to shut that person out of all your accounts to stop them from doing any more damage.

Also, beware of scammers attempting to gain access to your password by pretending to be from a company you do business with. The thief may call or send an email asking you to provide your password for a variety of purposes, such as technical support or account verification. No company will ask you for your password. The real company already has this information and will never ask for it for any purpose. If someone asks you to provide it, you're probably communicating with a scammer. Do not provide your password. Hang up or delete the email requesting it.

CHAPTER 4

FREE WI-FI

"Thank you for your business. See you next time!" Daniela said from behind the dark wood counter.

John smiled at the barista, picked up his coffee, and sat in an available leather chair which squeaked under his weight as he settled in. Though it had signs of wear, the brown Tuscan armchair was comfortable and inviting. It contrasted sharply with the plain, utilitarian furniture he had at his own apartment, where any prolonged sitting caused discomfort.

John savored a sip of the smooth, mocha latte goodness and set it on the brushed metal coffee table in front of him. He removed a black satchel from across his shoulder and extracted a silver, state-of-the-art laptop he had purchased online only a month ago. The marvel of modern technology activated almost instantly when he pressed the power button.

The lunch crowd grew at a steady pace, and soon the shop would be standing room only. John gazed at the other patrons, noting their keen, preoccupied interest in their mobile devices. Customers ignored everything else around them, including John. The self-taught programmer smiled at the scene, and with a few short keystrokes, he activated a special program of his own creation that automatically opened a wireless Internet connection named "Coffee Bay free customer Wi-Fi" for others to access.

As he continued watching the crowd grow, John took several large gulps from his latte. The mouthwatering liquid invigorated him, enhancing his sense of anticipation as patrons accessed his free Wi-Fi.

When the crowd thinned an hour later and there were more empty seats than occupied ones, John shut down his program, packed up his laptop, and moved toward the exit, tossing his empty cup into the waste bin as he walked by.

"Thank you," Daniela said. "See you next time!"

John smiled and nodded. "See you then!" He thought about asking her out, but that was a matter for another time. For now, he had too much work to do sifting through the data his computer program had siphoned away from Coffee Bay's patrons as they surfed the Internet through his network. Perhaps if he had the good fortune of stealing enough money from their online accounts beyond what he needed for his European vacation, he might ask Daniela on a dinner date to Le Crème, an expensive restaurant John had wanted to visit since it opened ten months ago.

FREE WI-FI MIGHT COME WITH A HEAVY PRICE

There are many wireless Internet hotspots that allow users to access the Internet for free. While these connections offer a way to stay in touch with the world, they could also offer a hacker a way to get in touch with your personal information.

Hackers have the capability of setting up their own Wi-Fi connections to capture data. They will make the name of the connection tempting for others to access, such as the free Wi-Fi lure used by John in the example above. The hacker may also use names of familiar businesses near the signal, such as "Glenn's Sandwich Shop free Wi-Fi," to fool people into thinking that the connection is safe since it's from a trusted name. Whatever you type into your computer while connected to the Internet through free Wi-Fi, you risk sharing that information with the deceitful person.

A hacker can use your connection to their "free" wireless network to monitor your digital conversations with others, obtain your login information for bank accounts and digital stores, gain access to your social media accounts, and record anything else you share across the Internet, such as documents, photos, and videos. That free Wi-Fi becomes a window into your life when it's controlled by a hacker.

The best way to avoid sharing your personal information through a free Wi-Fi connection with hackers is not to use the connection. If you must tap into free Wi-Fi, don't access anything online that requires an account name and password. Limit what you access through a free wireless connection to non-sensitive information such as sports scores, headline news, or horoscopes. This will help keep your personal information secure and prevent hackers from accessing your accounts.

Think of free Wi-Fi as a piece of cheese in a mousetrap. The bait may be tempting, but the punishment for accessing it may lead to a lifetime of regrets.

Pro tip: Only use free Wi-Fi to access information that you would share with anyone in the world.

Besides creating their own Wi-Fi connections, hackers may also gain access to legitimate Wi-Fi Internet connections offered for free by businesses. Many of these businesses use weak passwords that can easily be acquired by hackers. A business might also offer the Wi-Fi password freely to anyone who asks. If the password is easily accessible to anyone, your data might be at risk if you use the connection. If a skilled hacker acquires access to these systems, they may gain the ability to monitor many functions performed by customers of the business through that connection.

There are steps you can take to use free Wi-Fi and minimize the chances of your personal information falling into the wrong hands. Before logging into a free connection, verify the authenticity of the connection. To verify authenticity, ask an employee at the establishment for the exact name of the network connection. Do not log into anything other than a connection that matches the EXACT spelling of the network name. A hacker may try to fool you into logging on to a fake network by closely matching the name of the real connection. Don't be fooled. Unless the name of the Wi-Fi connection you see is the one the employee gave you, avoid it.

When logging into a Wi-Fi connection, look for "https://" in the web browser (URL) bar. The "s" means that your connection is secured and the information you access is encrypted. Don't log into any account or share sensitive information through a free Wi-Fi network unless your connection is encrypted. While it may not be entirely foolproof in preventing a hacker from gaining access to your data, it's an option when no others exist.

To reduce the risk of your personal information falling into the wrong hands when accessing the Internet on the go, use a data plan through a cellular network provider. The connection may not be free, but your data privacy is worth far more than the hidden cost of a free signal.

CHAPTER 5

EMAIL SCAMS

"Aren't you coming to bed?" Brad called out from the bedroom.

Jill adjusted her position on the hardwood chair at the kitchen table and clicked open her email account. "Just a minute, sweetie. I want to see if Jeremy sent the final estimate for the remodel."

"Don't take too long. You know I don't sleep well without your goodnight kiss."

Jill smiled at the loving words. "You'll get even less sleep if I'm worried about the project coming in over budget. You know how I can't sleep when I'm anxious."

Brad remembered when they waited for word on the offer for their home three months ago. Jill tossed and turned the entire night in nervous anticipation, keeping him up along with her. He thought it best that she received her peace of mind, so he could avoid the necessity of drinking six cups of coffee the next day to stay somewhat alert. "Take your time. I'm not going anywhere."

"I'll make it up to you when I get there," Jill promised.

While poking through her emails, she found the one she was looking for. When she read its contents, she cheered in excitement. "They met our budget. It looks like we get to replace the cabinets after all!"

"That's nice," Brad commented. "Can I get that kiss now?"

"Be right there." Before she closed out her email, Jill spotted one from her bank. She opened it and read about a critical security upgrade that required her to verify her information. In her excitement with the remodel, Jill quickly clicked the link, typed her login information, and received a thank you message for helping her bank improve customer security.

Jill closed her laptop and moved to the bedroom, eager to celebrate the installation of the cabinet set of her dreams. Not long after she and Brad fell asleep, a thief used the account information Jill had typed into the fake banking website to log in to the real site. The career criminal used her new access to steal every dime the happy couple had set aside for their dream cabinets.

EMAILING YOUR LIFE AWAY

Email is a great way to stay connected with family and friends. Unfortunately, it's also a popular tool in a scammer's toolkit to steal your personal information, hijack your computer, or worse.

Scammers have become more creative in accessing your personal information, thanks to modern email technology. These scoundrels can specifically target your email address or a large collection of email addresses through a distribution list they either assembled themselves or purchased from other scammers. However a scammer obtains your email address, they have one of two goals in mind: to obtain your personal information or to corrupt your computer.

Email scams represent one of the greatest threats to your finances and personal information security because they're inexpensive to distribute, easy to use, and hard to trace back to the thief. This chapter includes many examples of actual email scams used by thieves to provide you with the resources needed to identify when you're being targeted for an attack. Study them carefully and pay attention to how a thief tries to get you to download a file or click on a link. Learning how to spot email scams can significantly increase your chances of avoiding them.

In an email scam, thieves might urge potential victims to verify their account information, as in the story above with Jill and Brad. The scam email might also encourage the recipient to take advantage of a special offer or act to avoid a negative situation. The email instructs the recipient to click on a link embedded in the text or to download an attached file. This process, in today's internet-driven world, is known as phishing.

When scammers phish, you are the target, and they're using your fear, concern, or greed as bait.

Pro tip: Never click on a link or download attached files contained in any email, no matter who sent it. It could be a trap created by a scammer, and you might inadvertently give up your personal information or access to your computer if you follow the email's instructions.

If you want to log in to your financial account online, manually type the website address into your browser. While you're on the site, bookmark the location in your browser to make it even easier for you to access next time.

An individual who clicks on a link in a scam email might be directed to an authentic-looking fake website. These sites can look very convincing and may be difficult to distinguish from the real thing. The link might also direct a person to a website that injects malicious software into their computer. Either result is great news for a scammer and bad news for the unlucky clicker.

Scammers generate millions in revenue each year from people who believe their deceitful emails. Anytime you click on a link contained in an email, you risk becoming a scammer's next victim, like a mosquito to a bug zapper. The email might make a link look tempting, but if you click it, you risk having your financial accounts and more zapped.

Additionally, be sure to correctly type the address of the website you intend to access into your browser. If you misspell it, you may end up at a site designed to look like the real thing but exists solely for the benefit of thieves who crave the information they want you to release to them. Always verify the site address you want to access to ensure it's the real thing before typing in personal data. Remember to verify, verify, verify before giving your trust to any website.

As promised, here's an example of a fake email designed to lure you into giving up your personal information. I received this one from a scammer posing as a prominent bank (I've italicized obvious grammatical errors typical in emails of this nature):

"Dear XX Bank customer,

XX is pleased to notify our online banking customers that we have successfully upgraded to a more secure and encrypted SSL servers to serve our esteemed customers for a better and more efficient banking services in the year 20XX.

Due to this recent upgrade you are requested to upgrade your account information by following the reference below, using our new secure and safe SSL servers.

To validate your online banking account, click on the following link:
http://onlineservices.XX.com/auth/AuthService?action=presentLogin

This email has being send to all our bank customers, and it is compulsory to follow as failure to verify account details will lead to account suspension.

Thank you,
XX Online Banking Security Team."

    This scammer was attempting to get me to "validate" my account information by using scare tactics. It's a powerful trick that scammers use to great effect, and it's one you must be prepared for if you receive such a threatening email. If the email appears to be from a bank you do business with, stay calm and call the company directly using contact information from your bank statement. Never use contact information provided in the email, as it could put you in direct contact with a scammer.
    There are several indicators in this email that suggest it's a fake. The first is that the sender didn't include my name or account number anywhere in the content. The scammers didn't have my information. Most scam emails won't contain any specific information about you except your email address. That's all they know, and it's a dead giveaway that they don't have an existing relationship with you.
    Another giveaway is the poor grammar at the end of the

email. Phrases like "This email has being send to all..." indicate that either the bank can't afford an editor for important emails or the scammer has a limited grasp of the English language. There are individuals, both foreign and domestic, who want a piece of your assets, and it's up to you to identify their treachery. Using bad grammar is one of these identification methods. A major company will avoid sending poorly written material, so if you receive an item that contains errors, you might have been contacted by a scammer. Act accordingly.

Here's another example of an email filled with errors:

"We recently have determined that different computers have logged onto your Online Banking account, and multiple password failures were present before the logons. We now need you to re-confirm your account information to us.

If this is not completed by Octomber 17, 20XX, we will be forced to suspend your account indefinitely, as it may have been used for fraudulent purposes. We thank you for your cooperation in this manner.

To confirm your Online Banking records click on the following link: http://www.XX.com/IdentityManagement/

Thank you for your patience in this matter.

XX Corporation Customer Service"

Thieves don't have to be bright to steal from you—just lucky. Once again, we see poor grammar and bad spelling in such an important email. For instance, the word "Octomber" should be "October," and "manner" should be "matter." The "company" also sent this same email to my account three different times over the course of a week, each with different expiration dates.

Have you ever heard the expression, "if at first you don't succeed, try again?" That's exactly what these thieves excel at. They attempted the same trick again, but this time with a different bank. Instead of [Bank Name], they tried using [Credit

Union Name]. I've never heard of this credit union before, but if it's being used in a scam, it's possible that it might exist somewhere. Here's the content of this notification:

"Dear XX Services Credit Union client,

The XX Services Credit Union disable you account. After three unsuccessful login attempts, your account was temporarily disabled until further investigation. You must reactivate your account at XX Services Credit Union immediately, or you wont be able to use your card again.

Once you have completed these steps, we will send you an email notifying that your account is available again.

Sorry for any inconvenience this may cause and thank you for your patience.

To continue please click the link below:
http://XX.cyberbranch.com/cgi-bin/hb/nph-balance.pl

The purpose of this verification is to ensure that your bank account has not been fraudulently used and to combat the fraud from our community. We appreciate your support and understanding and thank you for your prompt attention to this matter.

Copyright 20XX XX Services Credit Union. All Rights Reserved."

Scammers will adjust their emails to try different financial institution lures, hoping that one of them will get you to bite. The part I found most ironic about this email scam is its attempt to "combat the fraud from our community." Reporting this email to the Federal Trade Commission would indeed be a great start to that end. Once again, scammers are attempting to instill fear and concern in their prey, relying on the combined effect of these elements to press their target into quick action. Don't be fooled by these scoundrels.

I found another example of this type of fraud in an email received by an acquaintance. In it, the email presents a fake transaction from an online payment site to make her think someone had accessed her account and made an unauthorized purchase. A convenient link at the bottom of the message encouraged her to log in and file a complaint with the payment site if the transaction was not authorized.

Whoever sent the email was not trying to protect her interests. The person was attempting to gain access to her account by pretending to have already gained access to it, hoping to lure her into a panic so she would act to block future unauthorized transactions. If she had taken the bait, the scammers would have been able to capture her login information and gain access to her account.

Fortunately, she was wise to their scam and reported the incident to the payment site. If you experience something like this, be cautious, be skeptical, and be vigilant.

This next email is similar to the one my acquaintance received but has various additional elements to make it look authentic. I've replaced the names and addresses used in the original email.

Company Dispute : Your **Company** payment has been hold

Company customer service

Jul 16 at 4:18 AM

To youremailaddress@yourwebsite.com

This message contains blocked images. Show Images

Change this setting

Company logo

16 Jul   00:30:25 BST
Transaction ID: 87N248087Y457901U

Dear **Company** Customer ID: 5090923,

You sent a payment of $79.00 USD to
We've asked the seller to hold the item(s).

Dispute this transaction. It's important to let us know because it helps us make sure no one is accessing your account without your knowledge.

Seller
sellersemailaddress@website.com

Delivery address – confirmed

waterlooville
PO7 6bt
United Kingdom

Note to seller
"This is a Birthday gift, so send it today please"

Dispatch details
The seller hasn't provided any dispatch details yet.

Description	Unit price	Qty	Amount
Excellent CANON PowerShot A640 10.0MP Digital Camera From TOKYO JAPAN Item Number 171841425133	$79.00 USD	1	$79.00 USD

For more information about fees, see our User Agreement.
Issues with this transaction?
You have 180 days from the date of the transaction to open a dispute in the Resolution Centre.

Questions? Go to the Help Centre

Get verified – Pay with your bank and you're protected against unauthorised payments sent from your **Company** account. Log in and click the Unverified link below your name.

Please do not reply to this email. This mailbox is not monitored and you will not receive a response.

Copyright © 1999-2015 **Company** All rights reserved.

(United States) S à r.l. et Cie, S.C.A.
Société en Commandite par Actions
Registered Office:
RCS California B 118 349

Email ID PP843 - 38e379729732b

Postage and packaging		$10.00 USD
Insurance - not offered		----
Total		$89.00 USD
Payment		$89.00 USD

This charge will appear on your credit card statement as "**Company** *OXALISEXP*"
Payment sent to sellersemailaddress@website.com

This scam is more sophisticated and professional-looking than all the others presented thus far. It took thought and time to craft an authentic-looking email in a genuine effort to make someone believe it's real. A recipient's first reaction upon seeing it might be to click on the included links to dispute the charge. Don't do it. The hapless clicker will be directed to a fake company website that looks almost identical to the real one. If someone types personal login information into the fake site, the scammer would gain access to the email recipient's real account and begin making actual purchases.

As mentioned above, one of the tell-tale signs that this email is from a scammer is that it doesn't contain the account holder's name anywhere in it. Also, the "Customer ID" is not accurate. All the scammer knows about the owner of this email account is the email address itself. They are relying on the email recipient to provide more useful information.

Does the fact that the fake transaction in this email originates in a foreign country indicate it's a scam? Not necessarily. Thieves infest all corners of the planet, and it's possible someone in another country could gain access to your credit card or login information for a website you frequent. That's why you should make sure this is a scam email before deleting it.

To verify the authenticity of the "dispute," open a fresh page in your browser and type in the company's website. DO NOT click on anything in the email. You can log into your account from the actual website and check to see if the purchase is genuine.

Many companies have a fraud prevention email address to which you can direct any phishing scams involving the company. Find the fraud prevention email address on the company's website and forward the scam email to it. Delete the scam email afterward.

Scammers frequently pretend to be from financial institutions, and in the example below, a scammer attempted to get me to click on a link by stating I have a new rate notice:

"From: Well-known bank <contact@notbankaddress.com>
To: my email account
Subject: Rate notice for me

Hi XX,
This is your new rate notice.
Please use the link shown below to get your latest rates.
Access the latest rate here. (<------- this text contained a

clickable link)

Sincerely,
Well-known bank"

Banks do send their customers notifications about different events such as new statements, potentially unauthorized charges, and other topics. However, they don't use return email addresses that have nothing to do with the company. The sender of this email used an address that doesn't belong to the company it pretended to be. This scammer only used the name of a well-known bank to gain credibility, hoping to convince someone to click on the embedded link. Remember, never click on an embedded link in an email, no matter who sent it.

In another type of email scam, a scammer sends an email claiming to be from a well-known shipper. The scammer will copy authentic logos from the shipper's website and paste them into the email to give it a measure of authenticity. The message will try to convince the recipient that the company attempted to deliver a package but was unable to do so. It might also warn the recipient that insufficient fees were collected for delivery and the package will be returned unless those fees are paid. The email will likely include an attachment for you to download, such as a printable label, or a website link to take action.

Do not download anything from a scammer or click on any link. If you do, you risk handing over passwords, account information, and other valuable personal information that a scammer can and will use against you. Clicking on an embedded link could also open your computer to attack from a virus.

Here's an actual example of a message I received from a scammer claiming to be from a well-known shipper:

"Dear, XX

Courier was unable to deliver the parcel to you.
Please, download Delivery Label attached to this email.

Yours trully,

XX XX,
Sr. Operation Agent."

In this example, the misspelled word "trully" is a clear indication that the email is not genuine. Additionally, while the sender's email address may have included the company's name in the username (before the @ symbol), the actual domain (after the @ symbol) was something entirely different. A scammer can create an email username that looks like anything they want, such as BigScammer, BogusEmail, or Rob.U.Blind. You can't rely on scammers to use such obvious names, but you can check out the domain part of the address to see its true origin. A scammer's username might include your bank's name but have an obscure domain name like @lugmondoni.it.

When you receive scam emails, do not email the scammer to demand removal from their mailing list. If you send an email to scammers, they will know they've reached a live person. They will not only send even more scams your way, but they may also share your information with others to let them know they've hooked a live person. All it takes is sending the right bait to lure you into their clutches, or so they think. Never respond to a scammer's phishing attempts, including clicking on a "Click here to be removed from our mailing list" offer. It's a trap you don't want to fall into.

Some scammers want to lure you into other types of traps with a financially tempting communication. I received the example below from a "staff" member of a financial firm in a foreign country:

"Dear Sir,

I am Mr XX staff of a financial firm in South East Asia and i am contacting for a good proposal that will benefit both of us if you are interested, please reply back.

You are my first contact, and I am contacting you because I need to do the deal with someone outside my country who is not known by my co staffs or friends, not that is a risky business please be rest that is risk free but it's not the type of deal you let someone around you to be aware of even my bank do not even know that I am contacting you as it will be a deal between me and you.

I will explain better when I get your response, I shall wait for days and if I do not hear from you, I shall look for another person.

Thanks,
Mr XX

This email is free from viruses and malware because XX Antivirus protection is active.
http://www.XX.com"

    Replying to this individual would be inviting trouble. First and foremost, there is no such thing as a risk-free investment. Check out the chapter on investment scams in this book for more information. The scammer also employed a few other tactics in this email to convince someone to reply.
    Besides presenting a chance for financial gain, the email created a sense of urgency by saying if I didn't reply, they'd find someone else who would. They also attempted to create a false sense of safety and authenticity by including a section at the bottom of the email, indicating it had been scanned by virus software and is free of viruses and malware. Nothing is safe about this email.
    Beyond the content of the email, think about the sender for a moment. How would someone in "South East Asia" know me? They wouldn't. They sent this to a massive list of email addresses, hoping someone bites. When a person replies to inquire about the deal, the scammer will either attempt to gain financial account information or convince the respondent to send money for whatever reason. Never reply to these emails.
    Scoundrels may also attempt to impersonate someone you know to get you to click on a link in an email. The thief may compromise the email account of an acquaintance and use that person's contact list to send phishing emails to everyone on it. A

recipient of such an email may see the familiar name of the sender and click on a link or download a file in the email. That is why I suggest you never click on a link or download a file in an email, even if it's from someone you know. The only exception would be if you've already spoken to the individual and know that person is sending you a link or file you want to receive. Otherwise, don't click or download anything in any email, even from friends and loved ones.

Here's an example of an email I received from a "friend."

"From: Name of person I know <oddname@emailaddress.net>
To: My name <myactualemailaddress@emailaddress.net>
Subject: from name of person I know

hey. how are you? http://unfamiliarwebsite.net"

The scammer who sent this was trying to get me to click on the link. To do that, they used the name of an acquaintance twice and asked an innocuous question. In this case, the email address of the sender did not match the actual email address of the person I know. If the scammer gained access to my acquaintance's account, they have no idea how long they will have access to the stolen email account before the real owner shuts it down. To avoid that issue, the infiltrator will extract every piece of useful information from the hacked account and use an anonymous account they control to initiate electronic stealth attacks. It's a clever way to avoid getting caught.

The scammer might have also tapped into their target's social media account, either by hacking it or perusing publicly available content to obtain names and email addresses in that person's contact list. That's why it's important to avoid clicking on links or downloading files from friends and family unless you know in advance that someone is sending you something. The email might not be from the person you think. Also, avoid making your contact information publicly available on your social media account unless you prefer to opt in to scam emails.

If I had replied to the email from my acquaintance for any reason, the scammer would have known that the account belonged to a live, active individual and might have used other tactics to get me to click on a link, download a file, or simply sell my email address to other scammers. If you have doubts about the authenticity of an email, call the person using information not included in the email and make sure it's real.

You can limit the amount of spam and scam emails you receive by creating several email accounts and using them for different purposes. Create one for each of the purposes below:

- One for business purposes, such as utility companies, financial companies, etc.

- One for employment use, such as applying for jobs or corresponding with clients.

- One for use with your social media accounts.

- One to give to close friends and family.

- One to give out when entering contests, filling out surveys, or to give to someone you don't want contact with in the future but hate saying "no" when a person asks for your information.

Pro tip: Give each email account its own, separate password and don't co-mingle accounts. Use one email account for a specific purpose and stick with it.

If one email account becomes compromised by a hacker or is bombarded by an avalanche of spams and scams, create a new email account and switch correspondence to that account. Compartmentalizing different types of emails to their own separate accounts makes the process of switching to a new account less difficult. It will also ensure that if a scumbag hacks into one of your accounts, they only have access to the content within it and not all your correspondence from other accounts.

There are criminals in this world who will do whatever it takes to fool you into giving them what you have. Be aware of their methods of attack and don't let them take anything from you. You may report any incidents of fraud to the company the scammer is impersonating or to the Federal Trade Commission at ftccomplaintassistant.gov. If a scam email involves the Postal Service, report the scam to spam@uspis.gov.

Do what you can to fight back and hold these scammers accountable for their illegal and immoral actions.

CHAPTER 6

CLOUD STORAGE

Dean searched frantically for his phone, but after an hour of rifling through drawers, dirty clothes strewn haphazardly on the floor, and under every seat cushion in the apartment, he came up empty. He moved to his laptop on the frosted glass surface of the coffee table and flipped it open. When the computer finished booting up, Dean connected to his video chat software and called Bobby.

"Dean, how's it going?" Bobby asked.

"Not good. Did you happen to pick up my phone from the party last night?"

Bobby shook his head. "No, not me. Did you lose it?"

Dean sighed. "I think so."

Kylie sat down abruptly next to Bobby, pressing her body next to his. She kissed him on the cheek and turned to the computer screen. "Oh, hi, Dean!"

"Hey, Kylie. You didn't happen to see where I put my phone last night, did you?"

"You mean after you let Angela use it?" Kylie replied.

Dean looked confused. "Angela? I didn't give her the phone."

Kylie shrugged. "Oh. Okay."

"Wait, why do you think I let her use it?"

"Well, it has that green cover with an upside-down yellow triangle and a circle around it, right?"

Dean nodded and inched closer to the screen. "Yeah, that's it. You saw Angela using it? When?"

"Last night, silly. Weren't you paying attention?"

Dean shook his head. "No, I mean when did you see her using it last night?"

"It was just before we left."

"Why didn't you tell me?" Dean scolded.

Kylie tucked her legs under her rear on the overstuffed couch. "I thought you two hit it off and she was just borrowing it. How was I supposed to know?"

"Yeah, chill out, man," Bobby agreed. "It's not her fault someone else took your phone." He clasped Kylie's hand in his and smiled at her.

The rich, black leather couch squeaked when Dean leaned back against it. He ran his fingers through his brown, disheveled hair. "I'm sorry. I just spent $700 on it last week, and I didn't get the insurance."

Bobby puckered his face in a painful look. "Ooo, bad move, dude. Hey, maybe Kylie can help." He looked at his fiancée. "You work with her, right, sweetie?"

Kylie nodded. "She works in the cubicle next to mine. I can text her and see if she has your phone."

"If you wouldn't mind," Dean agreed. "I just hope she didn't take it to get back at me for turning her down."

Kylie paused her typing on the screen of her phone. "What do you mean?"

Dean rubbed the back of his neck. "Well, she seemed nice at first, but then she started to talk about her dream wedding and the number of kids she wanted to have. That's when she asked me how I'd tell her parents that I wanted to marry her if we got engaged. Did you know she already picked out the names of her future kids?"

"Seriously?" Bobby asked.

"Yeah. Chris, Jamie, and Stacy, just in case they were boys or girls."

"Wow. What did you tell her?" Bobby asked.

"She was moving a little too fast for me, so I told her I hoped she found the right guy someday. That's when I went to find you two."

Kylie set her phone down in her lap. "Uh, oh."

Dean looked concerned. "What do you mean, uh, oh?"

"I mean, she gets that a lot. You know, disappointed by her dates."

"What does she do about it?" Bobby asked.

Kylie accessed her phone and opened her social media

page. "She tells her friends about it online."

"Is that all?" Dean asked.

Kylie searched through the morning's activity on her phone. "Let's just say they're not very flattering to the guys."

Dean shook his head. "Great."

Bobby's eyes opened wide in shock while staring at Kylie's phone. "Aw, man. Did you leave the photos from Max's bachelor party last month on your phone?"

"I just got the phone last week. I haven't taken a single photo with it yet. Why?" Dean asked cautiously.

Bobby grimaced at the image on Kylie's screen. "Well, you must have had them somewhere. Angela just posted one on her page."

Dean sat up straight. "She what?" He searched through his memory to figure out how Angela could have obtained the private photos. The answer almost immediately popped into his mind. "Oh, no. The cloud. I just set up the storage account this past weekend."

"Well, you'd better shut it down fast before she posts anything else," Bobby suggested.

"If she has one, she probably has everything else already," Kylie said.

Dean accessed his cloud storage account on his laptop and quickly changed his password. "There. That'll keep her from getting anything else in it. I knew I shouldn't have stored my password in the darn thing, but I have so many freaking passwords as it is. I didn't want to remember another one."

Kylie giggled when a new image appeared on Angela's page. "I didn't know you were so...flexible, Dean."

Dean lowered his head in defeat. "Aw, man. Not that photo."

CLOUD STORAGE

Cloud storage is a popular way to keep files on the Internet, allowing their owners to access them anywhere, at any time. Someone who uploads a file to the cloud can access it later from a phone, tablet, or other device from any location with Internet access. Files on the cloud are available 24 hours per day, 7 days per week, with zero downtime. This is accomplished by storing data across multiple servers in multiple locations. While the convenience of being able to access files anywhere on any device is worth considering, the process isn't without risks.

As in the scenario above, if you set up a cloud storage application to access your account without having to type your password each time, someone might be able to obtain your private files if they gain control of your device. To prevent access, first set a passcode for your phone. This is your first line of defense. Afterward, set the cloud application to require your password every time it's accessed. If someone peeks over your shoulder to gain your passcode when you unlock your phone and then finds a way to steal the device later, or someone asks to borrow your phone to make a call, this second preventative measure should keep your cloud files safe. Be sure the cloud application password is different from the one to unlock your phone.

Just like any account that requires a password, a passcode to a phone can also be hacked if it's easy to guess. If someone gains access to your passcode, that individual can access your photos, videos, and applications stored on your phone. Make sure your passcode is not personally identifiable, just as you would with any other password. Don't use your spouse's birth date, wedding anniversary, or anything else that others can guess if they perused your social media page.

Besides gaining access to your cloud account through your phone, a thief can also compromise the computer system at the cloud company. If a criminal finds a way inside the company's system, or if a company employee decides to raid customer accounts, your data might be stolen. In addition to cybercriminals looking for a way into your files, the storage company itself may also access your files for technical support, security purposes, or other reasons outlined in its Terms of Use. Read the Terms of Use agreement before signing up for any cloud storage to help you evaluate the risks of storing your personal files on their servers.

An additional measure you can take to help decrease the risk of your personal information falling into the wrong hands is to password-protect important files before you store them on the cloud. The process isn't difficult, but it can become cumbersome to remember the passwords, especially if you have many files to upload. It's worth the extra step, however, since it adds an extra layer of protection that will help prevent someone from poking around your personal information.

Some computer programs, such as word processing, spreadsheet, and presentation programs, offer the option to password-protect your files. For other items, such as photos and videos, password options may not be available. To add a password to photos and any other files, insert them into a compression program that places them into a single, compressed folder. Type "file compression" into your favorite search engine to learn how to do this if you're unsure. When you compress the files into a single folder, create a password for that folder. You can now upload it to your cloud storage account with an additional layer of protection.

CHAPTER 7

VIRUS PROTECTION

"Why did we sign up for the cinema connoisseur's package again?" Oliver pointed the remote control at the television and pressed the up arrow for the 20th time in 30 seconds. "They keep showing the same movies every month. And forget watching regular channels. There's nothing to see there but infomercials and reality shows. What happened to quality entertainment?"

Karen laughed uncontrollably. "I'm sorry, dear. What were you saying?"

Oliver frowned and turned to Karen, who remained focused on her 22" computer screen without turning to face her husband of 34 years. Oliver sighed and set the remote on top of the flower patterned cushion next to him. With great effort, he stood up from the couch, using the sturdy armrest for support.

"I said, why are we paying for these channels when there's nothing to watch?"

"There's plenty to watch, dear. You're just not looking in the right places."

Oliver moved to the living room desk and stood behind Karen. He peered over her shoulder at the monitor and squinted at a video of a cat swatting at pink bubbles that formed atop a deepening pool of water in a bathtub. "What is that?" he asked.

Karen laughed when the cat slipped on the edge of the white, steel tub and nearly fell in. "What does it look like?"

Oliver raised a white eyebrow. "I don't see how that's funny."

Karen shook her head. "You never did have much of a sense of humor. Maybe that's why you can't find anything to watch."

"We're paying $220 a month for unlimited television

access, and you spend your time watching cat videos on the Internet. Why do I bother?"

Karen tilted her head and looked up at Oliver. His bald head gleamed in the late Saturday morning sunlight as the sun shone through the open window. "You're the one who wanted to catch up on all the television you missed while working full-time. I told you to take up painting when you retired. You used to love doing that when we first met. What happened?"

Oliver shook his head. "I guess I thought sitting on my rear for longer than 30 minutes for meals would be a nice change. I was wrong." He looked away from Karen's aged but beautiful face and stared at her screen. "Hey, click on that."

Karen returned her gaze to the computer screen and looked below the video at the comments. "Return of the Renegade Soldier from Kaldoon?"

"Yeah," Oliver confirmed. "Isn't that movie still in the theaters?"

Karen shrugged. "I've never even heard of it before."

Oliver's eyes opened wide with excitement. "I thought I'd have to wait another six months to watch that on a premium channel. Let me pull up a chair, and we'll watch it together."

Karen stood up from her black, ergonomic chair and gestured to the empty seat. "Don't bother. It's all yours."

Oliver rubbed his hands together and sat down in the chair. "Are you sure you don't want to watch it with me?"

Karen adjusted a lock of silver and gold hair behind her ear. "I'm sure. I'll get started on lunch. Have fun."

Oliver nodded distractedly as he clicked on the link to the video. When an hour and 45-minute long video appeared that displayed nothing more than a static image of multiple, inverted arrows and an instruction to click on a link in the description to watch the movie, Oliver obeyed.

A new window appeared on the screen instructing Oliver to download a specific video player to watch the selected movie. He continued following the instructions presented to him until a "Hard disk error" message popped up, telling him to restart his computer to clear the error.

Oliver muttered something under his breath and did as he was told. When the computer resumed operation, desktop icons disappeared, and a message popped onto the screen telling him to run a diagnostic scan. With a frustrated growl, Oliver clicked on the "Begin scan" button. After the program finished its scan, a new message appeared on the screen informing him that the computer was infected. It offered to correct the issue by downloading a malware removal tool for $69.95.

Oliver punched the air in front of the monitor. "Bah! Nothing's ever easy."

"What's that, dear?" Karen asked from the kitchen.

"Grab my wallet. The stupid computer has a virus and I have to buy a tool to get rid of it."

VIRUS PROTECTION

How important is virus protection? In the scene above, Oliver downloaded a virus when he tried to watch an illegal copy of a movie. If Oliver had virus protection software on his computer, it likely would have caught the malicious program before it had a chance to do any damage.

There are many virus protection packages available for purchase, which can make the selection process difficult. Additionally, if you search the Internet for virus protection software, you might end up with a virus that poses as virus protection software. If you're unsure how to find one or which one to choose among the many available, go to a brick-and-mortar store that sells computer software, preferably one that specializes in computers, and ask a store representative to help you select one. Not only will you be reasonably certain that what you buy will help rather than hurt your computer, but you can also get help from the representative on how to install it.

Before you take a trip to the store to pick out an antivirus package, check to make sure you don't already have access to one for free. New computers sometimes come with a 1-year free trial of an antivirus software package. That gives you the chance to see if the software works for you. If not, then see what's available at the store as an alternative.

Internet service providers may also offer virus protection for free as part of your Internet package. Call your provider and find out if this is an available option.

Besides protecting your computer with antivirus software, you should also make sure to update the software on your computer whenever there's a new patch available. Keeping software up-to-date ensures that you have the latest modifications that will correct any previously unprotected software vulnerabilities. Think of updating, or patching, software as fixing a hole in the pocket of your pants. Unless you patch the hole soon after it's discovered, you risk losing something you place inside it to someone who will use it for their benefit, perhaps even to someone who might cause you harm.

All software should be updated when there's a new patch available, but these are critical to keep bad actors from accessing your computer:

- Operating system (such as Windows, etc.)

- Web browser (such as Firefox, etc.)

- Virus protection software (such as Norton, etc.)

- Video chat software (such as Skype, etc.)

Updating software is not the same as upgrading it. Software developers offer updates to their products for free. This helps keep you safe from software deficiencies and protects the developer from lawsuits that might otherwise surface if the company fails to fix problems known to cause harm to purchasers. Software upgrades usually offer new features and capabilities that don't exist in previous versions. Upgrades cost money, updates don't. Update software whenever a new patch is available to keep your computer safe. Upgrade software whenever you feel the additional features justify the expense.

The process of updating software doesn't have to be a pain. In fact, you can set most software to take care of the task for you automatically whenever there's an update available, so you won't have to worry about it. Most developers will have an instruction manual, website, or telephone number you can call to get the help you need to update software. If you need assistance, go directly to the company's website or call the technical support line to determine how to do this. You can also ask a friendly representative at the brick-and-mortar computer store to guide you through the process.

If you receive an email informing you that a software update or upgrade is available for free, don't click on any links or download any files in the email. The Email Scams chapter in this book has more details on how doing either task can harm your computer. To verify if the email is authentic, open a fresh web page and type in the software developer's website. Click on the Support or Contact Us tab and ask the company if the offer is genuine. If not, delete the email.

Think of updating your software and running virus checks as going to a doctor. The process may not necessarily be enjoyable, but your doctor knows what to look for to help keep you healthy. A doctor can also spot potential problems before they have a chance to develop and identify small problems before they become big ones. Keep your computer healthy and prevent hackers from accessing it by giving it a regular checkup.

CHAPTER 8

MALWARE AND PROTECTING DATA

"Goodbye, Grandma!"

A 6-year-old girl wearing a stained, purple shirt and blue jeans turned to wave at her grandmother from the walkway outside. She gripped her mother's hand tightly as they made their way to a tan sedan parked in front of the contemporary single-level green house.

Mary smiled and waved farewell to her granddaughter from the doorway. She hadn't seen Isabel in two months and marveled at how much the young girl had grown in that time. Though the visit only lasted for three short hours, Mary appreciated the chance to babysit Isabel while the child still needed her care.

With a sigh, Mary closed the front door. A feeling of disconnected loneliness began to creep into her thoughts as she picked up Isabel's dishes from the coffee table. She made her way to the kitchen, remembering a time when her husband, Jack, would comfort her and make the separation from her daughter and grandchild more bearable.

That was a year ago, before Jack's stroke.

Mary deposited the dishes into the sink and made her way to the living room computer. She touched the mouse Isabel had used only a short while ago. Though the cold plastic held no obvious traces of Isabel's use, Mary could still see her granddaughter gleefully popping balloons on an Internet-based computer game.

With the press of a button, Mary brought her desktop computer to life. She intended to leave a message of thanks to her daughter on her social media account for the brief but enjoyable visit. Within moments, a frightening message appeared on the screen.

"Your computer has been locked!"

A sense of dread washed over Mary as she read the details of the message.

"Your computer has been locked due to suspicion of illegal content downloading and distribution. The illegal content has been classified as child pornographic materials. The downloading and distribution of illegal content, in whole or in part, violates U.S. federal laws."

The message went on to describe the fines and jail time Mary might face for violating the law. It also stated that Mary could avoid prosecution and have her computer unlocked if she paid a fine of $300.

MALWARE AND PROTECTING YOUR DATA

During her time on her grandmother's computer, Isabel performed an Internet search for a fun game to play and found an interesting-looking website. When she clicked on the link, she opened the computer to attack from a vicious malware program.

Computer users are seeing an increase in this type of ransomware attack. Ransomware is a type of malware that usually embeds itself into a computer when someone clicks on an unverified link or downloads a compromised file, and it always leads to bad results when it gets inside a person's computer.

The ransomware-generated message that appears on a compromised computer's screen is similar in all attacks: pay a fine/fee within a given timeframe or have all data on the computer deleted or permanently blocked. The screen may use one or more official law enforcement logos to grab your attention. It may use a variety of messages to make you think you did something wrong on the Internet, or it can get straight to the point and demand money for your data without creating an excuse. The screen will display instructions on the types of payment the program will accept, such as MoneyPak or Bitcoin, and it will require you to send payment by a certain date and time to gain access to your files again. Failure to comply will permanently deny you access to your files.

A legitimate law enforcement agency won't hijack your computer and make you pay a ransom to release it. If you broke the law, you'll receive a knock on your door, not a locked computer.

In addition to tainted links and downloads, dialog boxes might also pop up on your computer screen that will tell you to click it for faster computer performance, to download an important software upgrade, or ironically, to download the latest virus and malware protection. These boxes are designed to look authentic and make you believe they're from reputable companies. DO NOT click on anything inside the box. If you do, you may open a virtual door for a virus to infect your computer, steal your personal information, or cause damage to your files. To get rid of the box, click the X in its upper right-hand corner.

Despite your best efforts to secure your computer, a hacker or malicious program may still find a way inside it. Besides stealing your personal information or your money, some malicious software creators design their abominations to cause your computer harm just for fun.

There are programs that will infect your computer and corrupt your hard drive or cause damage that prevents you from accessing your files or your computer's operating software, without asking for money to repair it. You may lose important documents, family photos and videos, and other irreplaceable items if your computer becomes infected. Some hackers thrive on chaos and destruction. They seek to cause harm to others merely for the pleasure of doing it.

There is only one way to make sure you minimize the damage a hacker can do to your files: keep a backup copy.

One easy way to back up the data on your computer is to purchase an external hard drive. An external hard drive is like the internal hard drive installed on your computer, only you can detach it from your computer and keep it elsewhere. It connects to your computer through a USB port just like a flash drive but can hold a great deal more data than a typical flash drive.

When shopping for an external hard drive, select one that meets the size you need. How do you know the size you need? Find out the capacity of your computer's hard drive and buy an external drive at least as large to make sure it can hold everything on your machine. Many external drives contain built-in software for backing up your hard drive. This makes the process of backing up your data easy. Be sure to look for a drive that has this software.

After purchasing your external drive, pick a regular schedule to back up your files and stick to it. I prefer monthly backups, but you should select what works best for your needs. If a malicious program gains access to your computer and corrupts your information, you'll only lose the data you added to the computer in between backup intervals, which is considerably less than losing everything. This also gives you the option of reformatting the hard drive inside your computer to get rid of the virus without worrying about losing much personal data. Reformatting a hard drive is sometimes called a "nuclear option" for eliminating hard-to-remove viruses because it wipes out everything on your hard drive. Every software program you have, including the operating system, must be reinstalled when you "nuke" your hard drive. The process is lengthy, but it works.

Backing up your files is also a good habit to have in case a damaging non-virus-related event happens to your computer. Hard drives eventually fail, and you don't want everything you stored on it for years to be wiped out if you've never backed it up. There are specialists who might be able to recover information from hard drives that have crashed, but the cost range begins in the triple digits and might go higher, depending on the efforts needed to recover the data. The cost of backing up your data on an external drive is small in comparison to what it might cost you to have someone else recover your data, if it can be recovered at all.

Besides hackers, malicious software, and equipment failure, other outside factors might cause you to lose your data. Fires, floods, and break-ins occur all the time, and you never know when your home may be next. If you keep your files on a backup drive and place that drive in a fireproof and waterproof safe, you stand a greater chance of keeping all the electronic documents you spent a lifetime accumulating. You might also consider keeping the external drive at an off-site location such as an office, house of a family member, or a box in a vault at your bank. Be sure the external drive is password protected, just in case someone at any of these locations decides to gain access to the drive. Many external drives have security software built-in, so pick one that suits your needs.

CHAPTER 9

MAIL THEFT

Robert waited patiently for his dog, Bucky, to finish his business. The bright afternoon sun felt good on Robert's skin after spending the previous week cooped up in his office. The Miller account had taken more time to finish than he thought it would, and the early morning and late evening work marathons had prevented him from seeing the sun from anywhere other than a small window on his way to the water cooler. Taking Bucky for a walk on a beautiful Sunday afternoon was the perfect way to unwind.

When his canine friend finished his task in a grassy area along the sidewalk, Robert slid a plastic bag over his hand, dealt with the mess, and deposited the special delivery into a nearby trash receptacle. He moved to continue his path around the neighborhood and nearly collided with a woman pushing a stroller.

"Excuse me. I didn't see you," Robert said.

The woman smiled. "No harm done." She was in her mid-20s, wearing a tight, purple running outfit and designer headphones.

Robert peered into the stroller and saw a small child no older than 8 months of age. "Cute kid. What's her name?"

"Pam," the woman replied. "I really should be going. Her father will be back from the gym soon, and I want to finish my run before he does."

"Oh, yeah. Sure," Robert stammered. He moved out of the woman's direct path. "I don't think I've seen you around the neighborhood before. My name's Robert." He extended his hand.

The woman peered into the distance along the sidewalk before taking Robert's hand. "Lee."

"Good to meet you, Lee. This is Killer." Robert pointed to his two-year-old beagle.

Bucky looked at Lee and wagged his tail.

Lee raised her eyebrows in uncertainty.

"Just kidding," Robert added. "His real name's Bucky. Don't worry. He's harmless, unless you fear being licked to death."

Bucky panted.

"Sweet dog. Well, I'll see you around." Lee moved to adjust the audio player attached to her arm when Robert spotted several envelopes poking out from the top of a pouch on the back of the stroller.

"You should probably tuck those all the way into the pouch if you don't want to lose them. You never know who might find them if they fall out."

Lee quickly forced the envelopes deeper into the stroller pocket and out of view. "Thanks."

Robert nodded. "Sure thing. I wouldn't want a thief stealing all your formula coupons." He smiled playfully.

Lee gripped the handles of her stroller and strode forward.

"You're welcome," Robert said while staring curiously at Lee's back. He scratched Bucky behind his left ear. "Well buddy, it's just you and me again. What do you say to a nice lunch?"

Bucky looked enthusiastically at Robert and barked.

After passing several houses, Lee looked back in the direction she had traveled and spotted Robert and Bucky turning the corner. When they were out of view, she opened a mailbox shaped like a fishing tackle box and retrieved the previous day's mail. With casual ease, she stuffed the stack into the stroller's pouch along with the rest of the mail and strode forward to repeat the task for the remainder of the homes on the block.

DON'T LET THE MAIL BECOME AN EASY PATH TO YOUR VALUABLES

If you tend to leave mail languishing inside your mailbox for one or more days without checking it, you're inviting criminals to steal what might be inside.

You never know who might try to invade your mail or when

they might strike, but the longer your mail remains inside your box, the greater the chances that the contents will be pilfered by a criminal. Don't give scum the chance to steal what's yours. Remove mail promptly from your box every day. Also, when you mail a letter, don't leave it inside your box. Raising the red flag for your carrier to see when you have mail to pick up is an alert to thieves that you might have something worth stealing. Take your mail inside the Post Office and deposit it there to ensure it arrives at its intended destination.

When mailing a payment or sending money to friends and family, never send cash. This includes cash sent in birthday, anniversary, and other types of cards. If your mail is stolen, there is no traceable means to track cash. A criminal can use it almost anywhere, and there's no way to identify it as yours. Use checks and money orders to send payment through the mail instead. It increases the difficulty that criminals encounter when trying to use your money and provides a traceable means to figure out who the money really belongs to.

When sending checks in the mail, it's possible that a criminal might try to chemically remove some of the ink you used to write on the check and replace it with alternative information. This is called washing the check, and the criminal can place any information they like on the check, including an alternative recipient and a much larger amount than you originally wrote while your signature remains in pristine condition. To reduce the chances that what you write will be removed, only use pens with secure gel ink for checks and other important documents. The special ink makes the process of removal by thieves extremely difficult. Secure ink pens are relatively inexpensive and can be purchased at most stores and online. Type "secure ink pen" into your web search engine to find an instrument that's right for you.

If you plan on leaving home for a while on vacation or a work trip, don't forget to place your mail on hold with the Post Office before you go. As mentioned earlier, the longer mail remains in your box, the greater the chance a thief will get hold of it. Stop by your Post Office or go to usps.com to place your mail on hold until you return. It's a free service and may very well save your items from being stolen while you're gone.

Moving may or may not be something people look forward to, but thieves usually find it to be a rewarding experience, especially if you forget to promptly change your mailing address. When moving to a new residence, be sure to place a change of address with the Post Office as soon as you can. This will keep your mail going to where it belongs – with you. Filing a change of address doesn't last forever, though, so it's also important to notify the companies you do business with that your address has changed. This includes financial institutions, online stores, medical offices, magazines you subscribe to, and any other place that might send you something in the mail. Be sure to tell family and friends about your new address too, just in case they want to send you something special for your birthday.

In addition to mail theft, thieves are increasingly turning to packages left at doorsteps to satisfy their shopping needs. Just as in the mail theft scenario at the beginning of this chapter, a person may brazenly walk up to your door and steal packages left by a carrier before you have the chance to retrieve them. A good way to prevent that from happening is by choosing signature confirmation when possible. A package won't be left at your doorstep unless you're there to sign for it. That might not always be convenient for everyone, however, nor might it be an option when choosing a shipping method at an online store.

Another way to prevent package theft is to have items delivered to a more secure address or one where someone will be available to accept it, such as a work address, a friend's address, or a P.O. Box rented at a Post Office. These alternative destinations may significantly decrease the likelihood that your packages will be stolen. If these options aren't available to you, have the package company hold the package at its facility until you can retrieve it.

When you have no choice but to receive a package at your door, even when you're not there to retrieve it, you can still monitor the tracking number to keep an eye on your valuables. Package scans will tell you where your package is throughout the delivery process and when your package is delivered. This will allow you or someone you know to pick up the parcel before a thief has a chance to steal it. A free notification service from the Postal Service, called Informed Delivery, lets users sign up to receive texts or email alerts as packages move through the delivery network. The service also allows users to receive emails that contain digital images of mail arriving soon. That can be particularly handy in identifying what a thief may have stolen if a criminal breaks into your mailbox and steals your mail. Go to InformedDelivery.com to learn more about this service.

If you suspect that you've become a victim of mail theft, call the U.S. Postal Inspection Service at 1-800-275-8777 or go to postalinspectors.usps.gov.

CHAPTER 10

DOCUMENT SHREDDING

"Hey, Jeff. What's going on?" Philip asked over the phone.

Jeff sandwiched his phone between his ear and right shoulder as he continued to flip through paperwork. "Not much. Just going through some of my old mail. What's up?"

"Dude, I thought we were supposed to go see the movie. It's opening night."

"What?" Jeff paused in his search through billing statements. "Is that tonight?"

Philip sighed. "Yes, it's tonight. Did you forget already? We just talked about it a few days ago."

Jeff set the statements down atop the heavily stained, bare wooden kitchen table and switched the phone to his other ear. "Sorry, man. I'm just getting ready for the move to my new apartment next weekend. I have a few more boxes to pack up, and I want to get rid of anything I absolutely don't need. Did you want my VCR? It still works. I think."

"No, that's okay. Does anyone use those things anymore?"

"Definitely not me. Maybe the thrift store will take it."

"Yeah, maybe," Philip replied. "If they don't mind it taking up shelf space until it becomes a collector's item in a couple of decades. So, are we doing this or what? The movie starts at 7:10."

Jeff peeled the phone away from his ear and noted the time at the top of the screen. "Yeah, I can do that. I'll just box the rest of this junk and toss it before I go. The usual place?"

"How do I know where you throw away your trash?"

Jeff shook his head. "No, not the trash. The movie."

"Oh, yeah. Right. Do we ever go to any other theater?"

"Just checking," Jeff replied. "See you at 7."

"Don't be late," Philip warned. "You know how much I like watching the previews."

"Yeah, yeah. See you then."

Jeff slipped his phone into his jean pocket and grabbed a fresh trash bag from under the sink. He returned to the kitchen table and sighed at the mess of paperwork that nearly covered its entire surface. "Oh well, out with the old," he muttered to himself.

He positioned the trash bag at the corner lip of the table, and with a single brush of his hand, whisked the bulk of the paperwork into it.

On the way to his car, Jeff tossed the bag of paperwork and a box of old, broken artifacts from his awkward youth into the community dumpster. As he drove away to enjoy a night at the theater watching the seventh sequel of his favorite superhero film, a man in a dark jacket and black pants poked his head out of the dumpster and rubbed the top of his head. He scowled at the taillights of the car as it drove away before turning his attention to the newly deposited trash that fell on top of him.

"Jackpot!" the identity thief said aloud when he opened the bag of old account statements.

SHRED IT BEFORE YOU FORGET IT

Most people receive a healthy collection of items in the mail each week. Ranging from advertising mail and magazines, to credit card applications and billing statements, the collection can quickly become an overwhelming pile that threatens to make furniture vanish under its cloak of volume over time. Though it may be tempting in some cases to grab the entire stack and shove it into the waste basket, doing so could give others access to information about you that they shouldn't have.

Some thieves don't care how dirty they must get to steal your personal information, and dumpster diving is a good way to gain access to your sensitive data. Anything that has your name and address on it should be shredded before you toss it away. For larger items such as magazines, tear off any pages that have your information, and shred those pages. The rest can be tossed into the trash.

Pro tip: Anything that contains your name and address should be shredded before it goes into the trash. You never know who has access to your trash. The less information you make available to a potential thief, the better.

Items that are particularly useful to thieves include financial statements, utility bills, insurance documents, and anything else that contains information regarding your personal accounts. These may give thieves direct access to information about your accounts that can be used to obtain payment information, open new services in your name, and steal your identity. This is especially dangerous if the thief can pair the information from these accounts with other information they obtain through your social media accounts and other sources.

Documents such as credit card applications, mortgage applications, insurance applications, and other similar documents are almost as dangerous, even if you don't own an account at these institutions. These applications could be used by thieves to learn more about your financial situation, where you shop, where you bank, a ballpark estimate of your credit rating, and whether you're a tempting enough target for a financial attack.

Don't make yourself a tempting target for criminals to exploit. Destroy anything with your name, address, and account information on it before you throw it away.

CHAPTER 11

TELEPHONE SCAMS

"Hold on, I'm coming!" Paul shouted from the shower. Still partially covered in soap, he shut off the water, opened the curtain, and threw a towel around his waist. He had been expecting a call from his date, but this was much earlier than he anticipated.

Paul's wet feet lost traction on the tile floor as he stepped out of the shower. He began to fall, but his left hand found a solid object to grab and steady himself.

"Ah, man," Paul groaned as he realized he hadn't cleaned the toilet in two months.

When he finally reached his phone, it had already sent the caller to voicemail. He checked the number on the caller ID, but it wasn't one he recognized. Within a few seconds, Paul's phone buzzed, informing him that a new message was waiting.

"My name is Sandra Jackson, and I'm with the Internal Revenue Service," the message began. "We identified you through an audit of your tax records as owing money to the IRS. The amount must be paid immediately, or we will file a lawsuit against you. To avoid arrest and severe penalties, you must call us back as soon as you get this message to make a payment on your account." Sandra provided a callback telephone number before disconnecting.

Stunned, Paul sat on a vinyl barstool in front of the kitchen counter. He had used the same electronic tax filing software for years and never encountered a problem with it before.

"This has to be a mistake," Paul muttered aloud. He dialed the number provided by Sandra and waited for her to answer. On the third ring, Sandra picked up.

"Agent Jackson," Sandra said.

"Hi, this is Paul Anderson. You left a message for me to call you?"

"Yes. Our records indicate you owe us the amount of $296. You can pay by pre-loaded debit card or wire transfer. How would you like to pay?"

Paul shook his head in disbelief. "Hold on a second, this has to be a mistake. I received a refund this year. How could I owe more money than what I already paid?"

"Look, Mr. Anderson," Sandra began in a stern voice. "You owe us $296. If you don't pay us today, we're going to file a lawsuit against you tomorrow and call the local police department to have you arrested. Do you want that to happen?"

Stunned, Paul hesitated to reply.

"You can avoid being prosecuted if you pay us today," Sandra continued. "I can take your debit card over the phone if you act now. What's your card number?"

"I," Paul said hesitantly.

"Fine," Sandra said. "I'm calling the police to have you arrested."

"No," Paul replied quickly. "I just have to get my wallet. It's in the other room."

"I have other calls to make, Mr. Anderson. Make it fast."

Paul walked briskly to the bedroom and extracted his wallet from his pants lying neatly on top of the bed.

"Now, Mr. Anderson," Sandra insisted.

Paul fumbled his debit card out of his wallet, dropped it onto the hardwood floor, and picked it back up. "I got it. I got it," Paul said.

After Paul provided his card number to Sandra, he waited expectantly for her reassurance that he wouldn't be arrested.

"Thank you," Sandra said. "We'll let you know if we need anything else from you."

Before Paul could clarify what she meant by her statement, Sandra disconnected. He sat on the edge of his bed, bewildered by the interaction with Sandra.

HOW TO SPOT A TELESCAM

Do you know how to identify a telephone scammer when you hear one? It's not as easy as you might think, especially when a skilled scammer uses fragments of truth or intense emotions to lure victims into paying. The best way to avoid a telescammer is to never answer your phone unless you know who's calling.

If the caller ID on your phone doesn't display a number you recognize, let the call go to voicemail. If the call is important, the caller will leave a message. This will eliminate most of the scammers that might call you. However, some scammers will leave a message, just as Sandra did in the example above, so be prepared to give the message a sniff test.

A sniff test helps you determine if a message is genuine or if the caller is trying to scam you. Here's how to give a call a sniff test:

- If a message threatens legal action against you unless you make an immediate payment, it might be a scam.

- If a message doesn't mention your name but demands your attention for a time-sensitive offer, it might be a scam.

- If a message mentions a place you've never stayed at or a contest you never entered, it's probably a scam.

- If a message you receive has any of these elements, it fails the sniff test. Err on the side of caution and do not respond to a message that fails the sniff test. If you're unsure whether the message is a scam, locate a telephone number for the company or agency and call directly to find out. Never call a number provided by a potential scammer.

When you review a voicemail message, you have time to give the call a sniff test. If you're unlucky enough to have live contact with a scammer, they aren't likely to give you time to make an informed decision. Inflicting high-pressure tactics to force you into quick action is a common trick of the trade. It's also a tell-tale sign that what the person wants you to do isn't in your best interest.

There are two types of calls you can receive from a scammer:

- Cold call scams - the scammer won't have your name, address, or any information about you.

- Warm call scams - the scammer may have your name, address, and generic information about you.

While tricky, you can identify cold call scams by the caller's lack of information about you. A warm call scam may seem more legitimate as the scammer uses the few fragments of knowledge they have about you. They aren't "confirming" information they already have if they're asking you for it, and they certainly don't need it to verify your identity if they called you on your phone. Don't give them any information they can use against you.

Here are a few well-known scams to be aware of:

- A scammer enthusiastically congratulates you for winning a cruise or vacation.

- A scammer pretends to be from the IRS and tells you the agency is filing a lawsuit against you.

- A scammer pretends to be from local law enforcement and aggressively demands immediate payment to avoid arrest.

- A scammer pretends to be a distant relative or old friend in dire need of cash and pleads with you to wire money immediately.

Any call with these elements is probably a scam. If you're unsure and want to verify the call's authenticity, ask probing questions. For example, ask the "IRS agent" the amount of your latest tax refund or payment. An authentic agency can tell you this if they believe you are the person they seek. Ask the local law enforcement officer to confirm your home address. They should be able to do so if they genuinely believe they are contacting the right person. Ask the old friend or distant relative requesting money about their childhood pet (or something else you both should know). Persistent scammers will create excuses to avoid answering your questions and may use emotional tactics to stop you from probing further.

When you press a scammer for verification, they might get angry or try to bully you into paying. They might also use emotions to make you feel guilty for not believing them. Scammers will use your emotions against you to get your money. Don't give them the key to your wallet.

Like most email scams, telescammers often don't have more information about you beyond your phone number. Never provide your name or personal information to an unfamiliar caller. If an unrecognized voice claims to be your friend or relative, don't suggest names for them to latch on to. Instead, create a random name and ask if they are that person. If the caller accepts the name, hang up and never answer a call from that number again.

As soon as you identify a call as a scam, hang up immediately. Don't feel bad about hanging up on someone attempting to scam you. The individual you're hanging up on is likely a seasoned thief who has stolen from others before. Hanging up is an easy way to say no to the scam. Don't say goodbye or try to let the scammer down gently. Just hang up immediately.

Some professional scammers can manipulate caller ID information that appears on your phone. This has been particularly common with law enforcement scams. A local sheriff's department, city police, or other government agency might appear on your caller ID when a scammer calls. If you answer, they will threaten you with prison unless you send money immediately. No legitimate law enforcement agency will call you to demand money under threat of jail time.

Another prevalent scam involves a swindler calling or emailing to inform you that you failed to complete jury service. They will threaten you with jail time unless you provide personal information or money. Don't believe it. The clerk of the court will not call or email you to bully you into providing your social security number, birth date, or other personal information, nor will they demand money to avoid arrest. If you've missed jury service, the clerk will generally send correspondence through the mail, not an email or phone call.

If you receive one of these calls, hang up, find the number for the agency the scammer pretended to be with, and call to verify the call's authenticity. Don't dial any number the scammer provides but do report the incident to the real agency. Calling the real agency will also give you peace of mind that the scammer's call was indeed a scam.

Pro tip: The longer you're on a call with a scammer, the more likely they can manipulate you into giving them what they want. Hang up as soon as you identify the call as a scam without saying another word.

WHY DO TELEPHONE SCAMS WORK?

A direct conversation is the best way to grab a person's attention and hold onto it, which is why telephone scams are so effective. People can easily ignore mailed and emailed solicitations because they are impersonal. Nobody is standing in front of you or on the other end of a phone to tell you not to throw away or delete a solicitation. A scammer's most effective means of deploying a successful scam is through real-time contact with you. Scammers know how to shut down your arguments, move past your stall tactics, and do whatever it takes to keep you talking to them. They have the tools to pry open your wallet, so it's up to you to arm yourself with the tools you need to defeat them.

If you don't want solicitors to call your number, you can add it to the Do Not Call Registry with the Federal Trade Commission at donotcall.gov, but be warned: scammers don't care about the registry and will call you regardless if they think they can get your money.

Placing your number on a do not call list or blocking a scammer's number won't protect you from receiving calls.

Thieves are trying to illegally take your money and aren't afraid of getting caught because they've honed their skills to avoid detection. They use a large array of numbers to call potential victims and will simply use another number if you block one.

Only you can protect yourself from getting scammed. Avoid answering calls unless you know who's on the other end, and always hang up on someone who pressures you into something you don't want to do. You can also type the number that called you into your web browser to see if anyone else has identified it as a scammer's number. When you see that number on your caller ID again, you'll know exactly who you're dealing with and can act accordingly.

CHAPTER 12

FOREIGN LOTTERY SCAMS

Olivia waved at her neighbor as she walked along the stone pathway from her mailbox to her home. "Good afternoon, Tina. How are you today?"

Tina gave a thin smile, masking her pain. She released the handle of her garden sprayer. "Oh. Hi, Olivia. I'm doing okay. Just a little arthritis pain, that's all. I usually feel better when I water my flowers, but my doctor keeps telling me to hire a gardener for that."

Olivia paused 10 feet away from her mahogany, 4-panel front door with a wrought iron grill protecting a frosted pane of glass. "Maybe he's right. You don't want to overdo it."

"I can water my own garden," Tina insisted. "But enough about me. How's Alan?"

"He's taking a nap. We're going to dinner tonight, and he wanted to get some rest before we go."

Tina smiled warmly. "That sounds nice. I can't remember the last time I went out for a romantic dinner, but I do miss it."

Olivia felt a pang of guilt for talking about her dinner plans with Alan. Tina had divorced Rich seven years ago and never remarried. Though her children visited periodically, Olivia was Tina's closest friend.

"Would you join me for lunch tomorrow?" Olivia asked. "There's a new café in town I'd like to try, and I've heard the food is delicious."

Tina nodded. "I'd like that."

"Great. I'll pick you up at 11. See you then!"

Tina waved and squeezed the handle of her sprayer, resuming the task of watering her multi-colored annuals.

When Olivia reentered her home and moved into the kitchen, she thumbed through the day's mail. Buried between the grocery store ads and an overly generous collection of coupons was an official-looking letter from the Australian Lotto Commission. Curious, she opened the letter and read a notice from the managing director.

**"Dear winner,

Congratulations!

The Australian Lotto Commission is pleased to announce to you today that you are a winner in the final drawing of the Intercontinental Promotional Program. You were chosen in a random, World Wide Web computerized selection system drawn from more than 150,000,000 addresses throughout the world to promote the awareness of our international program designed to change the lives of millions of people worldwide.

Your ticket number B87-4916591 with winning numbers 34-12-16-1-23-4-41 has approved you to receive the 2nd category prize of $1,500,000. For the protection of your claim, this information must not be shared with the public to avoid abuse and fraudulent acts from unauthorized individuals.

To begin processing your lump sum payment, please contact Foreign Processing Manager Dr. Julian Morgan at the contact information below. Please include your reference number at the top of this letter on all correspondence."**

Astonished by the letter, Olivia carried it to her husband. She was about to wake him from his slumber when she paused. They had recently spent $4,500 to replace their home's air conditioning unit damaged in a hailstorm and another $1,500 to repair a broken water pipe in their front yard. It had been a tough year so far, and she didn't want to give Alan false hope that their financial problems were finally over.

Olivia returned to the kitchen and dialed the telephone number on the letter. When Dr. Morgan answered, he enthusiastically congratulated Olivia on her success and explained the process of collecting the winnings, including obtaining her credit card number for the small processing fee.

When Olivia hung up the phone, she walked with a rejuvenated spring in her step to the living room to tell Alan the good news. As she did so, the scammer pretending to be Dr. Morgan charged her credit card for the $2,000 "processing fee" and added Olivia's contact information to his suckers list. He would call her back the next day to collect an insurance charge needed to guarantee accurate allocation of the funds to her account.

NO, YOU DIDN'T WIN A FOREIGN LOTTERY

Many people dream of winning the lottery. It represents a chance to go on a fabulous vacation, pay off a hefty mortgage, or help struggling family members. However, the desire to win can also lead someone to financial destitution and a loss of independence.

Scammers use the lure of foreign lottery winnings and easy odds to convince people to send them money. The only winners of foreign lotteries are the scammers who walk away with millions in their pockets from people who thought their financial problems were finally over.

In the scam, an unscrupulous thief may contact targets through official-looking correspondence that lavishes congratulations upon the recipient for winning a foreign lottery, such as in the letter above. All a person must do to collect the winnings is pay a certain amount of money to the agency or official.

Alternatively, the target may receive an elaborate brochure describing the easy odds of winning a foreign lottery. The offer could also come in the form of an email or telephone call, but the content is largely the same. A target is lured into buying lottery tickets in a foreign country through the promise of better odds of winning than what he or she could receive from a local lottery. Once a person calls the number on the brochure and buys into the scam, that individual's contact information is placed on a suckers list. This list is a goldmine for scammers because it represents people who can be duped into handing over their money to thieves. People on this list will receive an endless avalanche of offers from other fake lotteries and scams. This is one list you don't want to be on.

Once someone buys foreign lottery tickets, even with a small amount of money such as $10, the scammer moves in to take even more from the victim. At that point, the scammer might contact the individual with the fantastic news that he or she just won the foreign lottery. The notice could be in the form of a telephone call from an enthusiastic person or an official letter offering congratulations on winning the prize. Once a target is filled with eager anticipation and a willingness to act, the scammer will tell the "winner" that the prize money will be released as soon as the person sends enough money to pay for the taxes on the winnings. The amount can also be described as a small processing fee, insurance payment, or other form of expense required before winnings can be disbursed.

Pro tip: It is illegal to play a foreign lottery in the United States. Those who do so are breaking the law.

Pro tip: No legitimate lottery will ever require a winner to send money to claim a prize. If you receive a notification that you won a lottery and must send money to claim your winnings, you are the target of a scam. It's a one-way transaction that will only transfer your cash to a scammer, and you'll never get a dime in return. Discard the notification or hang up the phone immediately.

Foreign lottery scammers may also try to trick you into sending them money by first sending you a check from the lottery commission. After you receive that check for your winnings, you would then be instructed to deposit the check into your bank account and wire a certain amount back to the scammer to cover miscellaneous fees or taxes owed on those winnings. While the money you wire to the scammer is real, the check you received is not. By the time your bank informs you that the check is fake, the scammer will have already received the money you sent.

Pro tip: Never wire money to someone with the expectation that the check they sent you will cover the transfer. The check you received is likely to be fake, but the money you send to the scammer is very real, and you'll never get it back.

Foreign lottery scammers may also ask you to fill out a claim form that requests your personal information and a bank account number in which you would like your winnings deposited. Never send your birth date, social security number, bank account number, or any other sensitive information to anyone that tells you you've won a prize in a foreign contest. It's a scam, and you don't want the dirt bag to score a huge payday courtesy of you.

In another pseudo-scam, false hope peddlers will offer foolproof systems to win the lottery. There are no programs that can guarantee you'll win any lottery, but you are guaranteed to lose whatever money you send to buy the program. Ignore any ads for products that claim to increase your odds of winning the lottery.

Don't let your excitement blind you to the obvious pitfalls of a scam. Never send your money for the promise of receiving someone else's money. It's a losing proposition and could leave you broke at the end of the day.

CHAPTER 13

CLASSIFIED AD SCAMS

"I'm coming," Gary said to the ringing phone in the kitchen. He shuffled to the counter next to the toaster and pulled his phone from the charger. "Yeah?" he asked as he removed his sweat-laden cap emblazoned with a unique baseball team logo and set it on the counter.

"Hi, Gary? It's Rhonda."

Gary grabbed a harvest-themed paper towel from a roller mounted underneath the cabinet and wiped his balding head clear of sweat. "Oh. Hello, Rhonda. How are you?"

"Just fine. Did you get my check in the mail?"

Gary opened a kitchen drawer next to the refrigerator and pulled out an express envelope. "Yeah, I did, but you sent too much." He removed a check from the envelope and read the figure. "This is for $1,310. I only wanted $810 for the bicycle."

"I wanted to make sure you have enough for shipping," Rhonda replied. "Do you know how much that will cost?"

"About $150. I got an estimate from the company the other day. That's not too bad, considering it'll be crossing six states to get to you. It would sure cost me a lot more than that to take it there myself."

Rhonda giggled. "I bet it would! I'm sorry about sending the extra. When you cash the check, could you send me the difference?"

Gary smiled at the phone. "Sure. No problem. I'll do that this afternoon. You're lucky I'm an honest guy. Someone else might have cashed the check and kept the rest for himself."

"I know. Thank you so much for helping me, Gary. I really appreciate it. This is my first time buying something from an Internet ad in another state, and I'm still learning. I'll remember to check the shipping cost next time, before I send payment."

Gary set the check onto the marble countertop and closed the drawer. "That's probably a good idea. You've gotta be careful these days with all those thieves out there. You don't want someone ripping you off."

"I appreciate that. I'm lucky I have such a gentleman looking out for me."

Gary blushed. "It's no problem at all. Say, why don't I get this check to the bank before they close and send you the rest. I'll head to the shipping company on Monday and get the bike sent out. You should have it by the end of the week."

"That would be wonderful. Could you wire the rest of the money to me when you finish cashing the check? I want to buy a rack for my car to hold the bike, but I sent you everything I had in savings."

"Sure, no problem," Gary replied. "Send me the transfer info I need, and I'll get to it when I finish with the bank."

"I'll head to the wiregram center now and text you the instructions. Thanks so much for doing this for me. I can't wait to get my dream bike, and I have you to thank for it."

Gary beamed. "Glad I could help. Let me know how you like it. It belonged to my wife, but it's been sitting in the garage since she passed the other year. I'm glad to see it put to good use again."

"It will be," Rhonda said. "I promise."

When Rhonda hung up the phone, she set it on her worn, wooden desk and smiled at a movie poster above her computer monitor of a man in a suit holding a cigar.

"You were right about greed. It's so very good!"

CLASSIFIED AD SCAMS

Classified ads are a popular place to connect sellers with interested buyers, but they can also be a place to connect scammers with potential victims.

Many people are attracted to the practice of buying and selling items through classified advertising, either in newspapers or online, to find great deals. While many honest people conduct business through classified ads, there are also those who are not so honest, such as the person in the story above. It's up to you to spot a potential problem before a thief can get hold of your money.

One common classified ad scam involves a buyer offering a cashier's check to the seller for an amount greater than the agreed-upon price of an item, as in the story above. There are two components to this scam: the check itself and the item for sale. The scammer may attempt to obtain the item for free by giving the seller a bogus check or try to receive cash from the seller, or perhaps even both.

To explain the excessive amount on the cashier's check, the buyer might claim it's for shipping charges, simply an accident, or needed to complete a separate transaction, and the scammer needs the seller to send the excess amount to a third party. Whatever the reason, the end goal is the same. The buyer/scammer will ask the seller to deposit the check into their bank account and wire the difference between the cost of the item and the amount of the check back to the scammer or someone else. The check may not immediately show up as a fake instrument when deposited. Some checks take up to a week or more to clear, depending on the financial institution. While the check is being processed, the scammer receives the wired money from the seller and moves on to try the scam on someone else.

Once the bank finds out the check is fake, the money the seller thought was in the account disappears. The bank is also likely to charge the seller a bounced check fee for the inconvenience of dealing with the bad check.

If a scammer is bold enough, the buyer may show up to purchase the item with a bad check in hand. The cashier's check looks authentic, and the seller hands over the item in exchange for the required payment. By the time the seller finds out the check is fake, the buyer is long gone with the stolen item.

"But it's a cashier's check! Isn't that good enough?"

The short answer is no. A scammer can create an authentic-looking check using a computer and printer. With modern graphic design software and a good color printer, a scammer can make any type of document look authentic. Just because a document looks authentic doesn't mean it is.

You can verify if a check is genuine by contacting the bank associated with it. If it's from a local bank, go to the bank and ask an employee to verify if the check is genuine. Don't feel bad about telling the buyer you want to verify the authenticity of the check before accepting it as payment. You don't know the person, no matter what the buyer tells you about their life. If the person gets mad about your insistence on verifying the money, don't close the deal. Thieves use anger and fear to force people to do what they want, and a thief wants you to hand over what you have for free. It's better to find another buyer than to let someone steal what you're selling.

Fake checks aren't usually connected to a local bank, making it more difficult for someone to verify their authenticity. While an out-of-town check can be a red flag that the payment isn't genuine, it might also be real. If you can't go to the bank's physical location, call the bank listed on the check using contact information you find online. Don't rely on the contact information on the check, as it might connect with the scammer's partner. Ask the bank over the phone if the check is genuine. If the buyer gets mad about your insistence on verifying the check's authenticity, walk away from the deal.

Just as selling an item through a classified ad can be dangerous, buying an item can be equally problematic. Some sellers may have ill intentions when it comes to doing business with you, and you could end up with far worse than a smaller bank account balance when dealing with a criminal.

A criminal posing as a seller might have a buyer meet at a location with little traffic or where few, if any, people will be around to witness the transaction. The seller will also ask the buyer to bring cash only to the meeting location. When the buyer arrives and shows the seller the cash, the thief will steal the cash and leave without offering the item in return. Some sellers may not want the buyer to report the theft to the police and could harm or kill the buyer to keep them silent.

Don't put yourself in harm's way. If you meet with a seller, do so in a very public, well-lit place. A local law enforcement station is a great location to conduct a transaction. Find the location of your local police, sheriff's department, or even fire station, and call the facility to ask if you can conduct the transaction there. Law enforcement and fire personnel want to keep you safe and will usually permit the transaction under normal circumstances. Once you obtain approval, call the seller and have them meet you at that location. If the person refuses or gets mad about suggesting the location, don't buy the item.

Pro tip: If a buyer or seller insists on a meeting location that makes you feel uncomfortable, don't conduct the transaction. Your safety isn't worth the item you're trying to buy or sell.

Pro tip: If you want to get out of a deal with a buyer or seller you're not sure you can trust, avoid telling the person that you think they are lying or attempting to scam you, especially if you think the person might hurt you. Some criminals are violent, and you don't want to risk injury or death by confronting the potential threat directly, especially if you're meeting in person. Over the phone, tell the person you've changed your mind and hang up. Don't answer the phone if they call back. If you're in contact with the buyer or seller in person, tell them you've changed your mind about selling or buying the item. If the person becomes angry and threatens you for refusing to finish the deal, tell them that you want to ask a family member if it's okay to make the transaction. Dial 911 on your phone, and either explain the situation to the operator or pretend you're talking with your family member if you can't get out of audible range of the individual. The operator will be able to identify the emergency from your conversation and provide you with prompts on how to proceed.

Just as buying and selling items through classified ads can be a rewarding experience under the right circumstance, so can finding a place to live. The experience may not be what one hopes for, however, if the person offering a property for rent is a scammer.

In a rental property classified ad scam, a thief will offer a property for rent through a tempting ad. An interested renter who emails the scammer will receive encouraging information about the property. Before the renter ever sees the property in person, the scammer may ask the renter to fill out an application that requests information such as their name, address, telephone number, birth date, social security number, employer, income, driver's license number, and more. The scammer may also skip this part and ask the potential renter to send the first and last month's rent, a security deposit, and perhaps other fees to secure the property. In either case, the scammer is looking for a quick reward from the renter and may claim that high demand for the property or some other bogus situation requires swift action.

Pro tip: High pressure is a thief's best friend. If someone pressures you to make a fast decision, it's not the right deal for you. Move on and find another property to call home.

A rental property scammer is devious in their approach to stealing money. Thieves may begin a scam by finding an existing rental property listing, copying the details of the property, and pasting the information on a classified ad website along with their own contact information. The thief could also find a property not currently listed for rent and use that information to fake a rental listing. The advertised listing price is likely to be under comparable rental rates in the area to guarantee a nibble from an interested renter. Once a renter nibbles, contact is usually conducted exclusively through email.

A rental property scammer will then claim to be out of the state or country on business, charity work, or on deployment with the military. Wherever the scammer claims to be, they won't be available to show the property. The scammer may pressure the renter into wiring money and possibly an application to secure the property.

If a potential renter sends money to a scammer, the victim could end up broke and without a place to live. If an application is also sent to the scammer, the renter could have their identity stolen.

To avoid rental property scams, don't deal with someone who claims to be out of the country or otherwise unable to meet you to view the property and asks for the transaction to be completed remotely. That's a red flag and shouldn't be ignored. If the rental rate the property owner requests is substantially below market rates for comparable properties in the area, that's another red flag. Unless there's a severe plumbing, electrical, structural, or other issue that makes the unit a less desirable place to live, it's probably a scam. If you're asked to wire money to a property owner when you haven't seen the property or met the owner/property manager in person, that's another red flag. Buying anything sight unseen has the potential to be a bad deal for a buyer. The same is true for finding a rental property.

Conducting a successful transaction through classified advertising is the reward of diligence and determination. Not every deal is what it seems, however, and what might initially look like a winning situation could end up becoming something far more sinister. Always use caution when conducting transactions through classified ads and verify that everything is what it appears to be before any money changes hands. Your money, and perhaps even your life, depend on it.

CHAPTER 14

WORK FROM HOME SCAMS

A blast of intense heat pummeled Sandy's face when she opened the oven door. Undeterred, she peered into the gloomy, yellow light and checked her roast.

"Perfect!" she said in delight. Cautiously, she extended her red, silicone-covered hands into the oven and extracted the heavy pan. After placing it on the ceramic cooktop, she removed her oven mitts and set them aside. Sandy closed her eyes and inhaled deeply. She could almost taste the delicious sensation that awaited her family for dinner.

"Is it ready now?" Gloria asked impatiently, with heavy emphasis on the word 'now.'

Sandy smiled at her 7-year-old daughter. Though it had been the fourth time Gloria asked the same question, Sandy never grew tired of hearing her daughter's voice.

"Just about," Sandy replied. "Go get washed up, and then help me set the table."

Gloria pouted. "Do I have to?"

"The sooner you get it done, the faster you can have dinner."

Gloria sighed. "Fine." She turned and trotted into the hallway.

Sandy added freshly diced tomatoes to a large, ornate plastic bowl filled to the brim with salad when her phone rang. She wiped her hands on a nearby kitchen towel and picked up a slim brick with a pink protective cover featuring a prancing pony.

"Hello?" Sandy asked.

"Hi, Sandy. It's Shawn. How are you on this lovely Saturday evening?"

"Just fine. My family and I are about to sit down for dinner though. Do you mind if I call you back on Monday?"

"This will only take a minute. You'll thank me for it later. I promise," Shawn cajoled.

Sandy hesitated briefly before continuing. "Okay. I guess I have a minute."

"Great! Al told me that you finished up the Mystery Shop Training program, and he was very impressed you did it so quickly. Congratulations! It sounds like you're a real go-getter. That's exactly the type of person we're looking for at Hammer and Reynolds Limited."

"Well, now that my kids are back to school, I could use the extra income. To tell you the truth, I'm eager to get out of the house again and get back to work. Daytime television isn't what it used to be."

"I hear ya," Shawn said. "Now that you passed the training, we can move forward with your certification. It's only $229, and it's a one-time cost. You'll easily make that back after your first mystery shop. If you wire the money first thing on Monday, we can get you started the very next day. Sound good?"

"I don't know," Sandy said hesitantly. "We don't exactly have a lot of money right now after paying for all of the back-to-school supplies. I thought certification came with the $249 training package."

"That's a separate charge," Shawn confirmed. "Without certification, we legally can't hire you as a mystery shopper. We don't want to break the law, and you certainly want to avoid wasting the money you've already invested. Do you have a credit card you can charge? You can pay it off with your first check."

A cacophony of clinking sounds behind Sandy startled her. She turned and watched as Gloria moved a collection of plates to the dinner table.

"If it helps, I can take your credit card information over the phone now, so you won't have to worry about it on Monday. I don't mind."

"I'm not sure," Sandy said. "We only use the card for emergencies."

"Sandy, after you get your first mystery shop payment, you'll not only have the money back on the card before the bank can charge interest, but you'll also have enough left over to buy any back-to-school supplies you weren't able to get. Do it for your kids. They're worth it. I have two of my own, and there's nothing I wouldn't do for them."

Sandy watched as Gloria placed silverware on the table next to the plates. "All right. Hold on. I'll get the card."

Shawn scrolled down the page of a website on his computer as he waited for Sandy to retrieve her card. He gazed longingly at the stylish design of a black and silver pair of smart glasses.

"All right, I have the card. Ready?"

Once he received the needed information from Sandy, he placed an order for the $1,200 smart glasses.

"Your certification has been ordered, and it's on its way. As soon as you get it, give me a call, and we'll get you set up for your first job. Sound good?"

"Yes, it does," Sandy agreed. "Thank you so much for your help with this. I really appreciate it."

"Hey, no problem. Well, you should get back to your dinner, and I think I'll do the same. Talk to you soon, and congratulations!"

As soon as he hung up the phone, he dialed a different telephone number.

"Hello?"

"Hey, Marcy. It's Scott. I've got another package headed your way, but I have a different address I want you to send it to when you get it. Do you have a pen handy?"

A WORK FROM HOME JOB OFFER MIGHT NOT BE WHAT YOU THINK IT IS

In the scene above, a duplicitous scoundrel employed two work-from-home scams to get what he wanted. He fooled Sandy into thinking she was going to be a part-time mystery shopper for extra income and charged her for the opportunity. He also duped Marcy into thinking she was participating in a legitimate work-from-home job, leaving her to take the heat from authorities when they eventually catch her sending items purchased with stolen credit cards and reshipping them to scammers at addresses outside the United States.

Many people are eager or even desperate to make extra money to help pay bills. They'll see work-from-home ads on the Internet, in newspapers, or even on signs taped to a neighborhood light post and presume an offer to be legitimate. While some might have merit, other work-from-home job offers are scams.

"But it's on a popular job website. It has to be legitimate, right?"

Not necessarily. Scams are easy to start, shut down, and start anew under a different name. If a job posting by a scammer is flagged as a scam on an employment or classified ad website, the offer may be taken offline, but that isn't the end of it. Scammers don't gather their toys and go home when they're caught doing something wrong by the school principal. They simply put on another disguise and deploy their scams again.

Scammers are persistent and earn their living by fooling other people into giving up their hard-earned money. With work-at-home scams, predators exploit desperation, offering hope to those who have none. They offer a lifeline to people willing to cling onto any ray of sunshine that beams their way. You must be vigilant to avoid becoming a scoundrel's next victim. Here are a few things to watch out for when dealing with work-from-home opportunities:

- Does the opportunity require you to give money to the person offering the job?

- Does the opportunity require you to convince others to sign up for the same job?

- Does the opportunity offer high compensation for very little effort?

If you answered yes to any of these questions, it could be a scam. Err on the side of caution, and do not proceed with the work-from-home opportunity.

Some people ignore signs of a potential scam and pursue such opportunities anyway. The allure of a lucrative income tends to cause some to throw common sense out the window. Don't let this happen to you.

The following work-from-home opportunities are notoriously popular with scammers:

- Mystery shopping – buy products or services and report on the experience.

- Stuffing envelopes – receive postage and content to place inside envelopes and deposit into the mail.

- Receiving and reshipping items – receive expensive items in the mail, repackage them, and mail to another address, usually outside the country.

- Building items – receive parts in the mail, assemble or craft the product, and ship it back to the company.

If you encounter one of these "opportunities," avoid it. It could be a scam.

While a small portion of work-from-home jobs might be legitimate, how can you tell the good from the bad? Start by doing your homework before responding to any such opportunity. I call it the Scratch and Sniff Test, and you'll see it used elsewhere in this book. Just like a scratch-and-sniff sticker, you'll have to apply an abrasive element to the veneer of the business you're investigating to see if what lies beneath the surface is what the opportunity claims to be.

Your first stop should be the Better Business Bureau at bbb.org. The free website provides company contact information, any complaints filed against a company, and customer reviews. It also lets you know if the business is BBB accredited and has committed itself to abide by a code of business practices. If the work-from-home company you found isn't listed with the BBB or has unfavorable information on the website, you're better off looking for another opportunity.

If the BBB cleared the company you're investigating, conduct a web search to see if there are any recent issues with it. Open your favorite web search engine and type the name of the company followed by the word "scam." If you find complaints against the company that suggest its offer is a scam, avoid it.

"The work-from-home company passed both tests. Is it okay to proceed with the offer?"

Maybe, but there's still a chance it might be a scam. A scammer could use the name of a legitimate business to fool others into thinking they're working with a reputable company. Go back to the BBB website and check the business's contact information with the information you have on the company. If they differ, use the BBB information to contact the company and ask about the work-from-home offer.

Should the company pass all your tests, your last line of defense is common sense. You've heard it before, and you'll hear it again: if the offer is too good to be true, it probably is. Listen to that nagging voice in your head if it warns you that something is not quite right with the offer. It might keep you out of harm's way.

If you've already been scammed by a work-from-home job offer, don't let the crook get away with it. Report the scam to econsumer.gov, your state's attorney general's office (go to naag.org to find it), and the Federal Trade Commission at ftc.gov/complaint. If the scam involved the mail, also file a complaint with the Postal Inspection Service at postalinspectors.uspis.gov. If the scammer took your personal information and is using it to assume your identity, go to identitytheft.gov and act to stop it.

CHAPTER 15

DOOR-TO-DOOR SERVICE SCAMS

Aubrey removed her straw hat, wiping her forehead with the sleeve of her pink and green plaid shirt. She glanced up at the gathering clouds and knew she didn't have much time before the summer storm hit.

The weeds had taken over her yard in recent weeks, nourished by the frequent rains. Aubrey had tried to keep up with them, but the relentless growth was more than she could handle in a single weekend. Her homeowner's association had sent a reminder to address the issue, but her busy schedule and overtime at work had kept her from tackling the problem until now.

If she didn't clear the weeds in the next few days, the HOA would fine her for non-compliance.

Aubrey grabbed her trowel and a plastic bag filled with pulled weeds, slowly standing from her crouched position. She winced at the pain in her knees and hobbled to the trash can set by the curb for collection the next day. After disposing of the bag, she shuffled back toward the house.

On her way, a man in tan pants and a green polo shirt with a landscaping company logo approached her.

"Hi, ma'am. I couldn't help but notice your weed problem. My name is Kim, and I work for Greenly-Benson Landscaping. We could help you out with that."

"I can handle it," Aubrey replied. "It'll just take me some time."

"I'm sure you can," Kim agreed, "but it looks like a big job." He gestured toward the sprawling weed-covered yard. "We've helped several of your neighbors with similar issues, and we can offer you a great price since we're already in the neighborhood."

Aubrey looked at the sea of weeds. "It's going to rain soon. I don't think you'll finish before it does."

"Ma'am, we work in all conditions. A little rain doesn't scare us."

Intrigued by the prospect of saving her knees from further strain, Aubrey asked, "How much would it cost?"

Kim surveyed the yard. "Normally, I'd charge $150, but since we're wrapping up another job nearby, we can do it for $120."

"I don't know. I should probably shop around first."

Kim nodded. "You could do that, but they'd charge you much more, and I can't offer this price unless we do it today. It's up to you, but if you want to save money, we should start now."

Aubrey knew she wouldn't finish the job before the HOA fined her $50, and finding another landscaper in time was unlikely. Given her constraints, she relented. "All right. Go ahead."

"Great!" Kim extended his hand, and Aubrey shook it, noting the smoothness of his skin. "You made the right decision. I'll grab my crew."

A nagging doubt crept into Aubrey's mind, but she brushed it aside as unnecessary worry.

Kim started to walk away but turned back. "I almost forgot. We need payment upfront. Our weed spray is low, and we need to buy more to cover your yard."

"All of it? You haven't even started," Aubrey protested.

"We use the best spray on the market. It lasts a year, unlike the cheap stuff that wears off in three months. If you don't want us to spray, that's fine, but you'll have weeds again in a week."

Aubrey knew the HOA would fine her if she had another weed issue soon. The promise of a weed-free yard for a year was too tempting to pass up.

"Go ahead and get the spray," Aubrey said. "I'll get the money."

When Aubrey returned with the payment, Kim thanked her and left to get his truck and crew. She never heard from him again. A week later, she received a $50 fine from the HOA for the persistent weed issue.

BEWARE OF DOOR-TO-DOOR SALESPEOPLE

In the situation above, Kim offered to help Aubrey with her persistent weed problem. To make the offer more tempting, he baited the hook with a reduced cost if she acted immediately. When Aubrey ultimately agreed, Kim knew he had her hooked. That's when he initiated the final stage of his objective. He asked for all the money upfront and presented Aubrey with an excuse as to why it was urgently needed, as well as the consequences if she refused.

Scammers lure their targets down a carefully constructed path filled with tempting bait and dangerous traps. Just as in many childhood fairy tales, evil thrives on the good nature of trusting people. Instead of an apple, candy treats, or porridge, morally bankrupt individuals offer empty promises and the illusion of trust. When someone knocks on your door, chances are, that person wants money from you. Are you prepared to say no?

If someone knocks on your door with the intention of obtaining money, the individual doesn't know anything about you. That person isn't your friend, nor are you likely to ever see them again once they leave. It's okay to say no to that person's offer. You are not obligated to buy anything from anyone. Don't feel bad about saying no and hurting their feelings. The person is there to collect money and will move on to the next house to obtain it, whether they receive anything from you or not.

Beware of the underhanded tactics used by scammers to push you into giving up your money. They might tell you about a roof problem you didn't know existed and warn you that if it's not taken care of immediately, very bad things will happen. They might say that other homeowners in the area have had issues with their furnaces, chimneys, or ducting and that yours should be inspected to make sure it's safe.

The salesperson might offer a free inspection for your furnace, chimney, air ducts, roof, and other items on your property. If someone shows up unsolicited at your door to offer a free inspection, they will find something wrong with the object under investigation, whether anything is actually wrong with it or not. If you politely say, "no, thank you," they will tell you about the dire consequences that await you if you fail to act.

The key element to the success of door-to-door repair scams is fear. The scammer will make you afraid of not getting the job done. Fear-mongering works on those without knowledge of a situation and is used successfully by scammers to take money from the uninformed. Does that mean you should know everything there is to know about every part of your home? Not at all. All you must know how to do is pull back the curtain of ambiguity to see what lurks behind it.

Scammers want to take your money now and will rarely wait to receive it. Why? Repeated contact with a potential victim places a scammer at greater risk of being discovered and arrested. It's similar to why a burglar spends as little time as possible in a home they are robbing. The longer the burglar remains in the home, the more likely they will be caught and sent to jail. To avoid being caught, the scammer will pressure a person into acting immediately and then disappear with a victim's money, never to return. Immediate action is a scammer's best friend and their greatest weakness.

If a scammer can't get what they want now, they are unlikely to return later to seal the deal. A good way to filter out scammers from legitimate businesses is to avoid taking immediate action. It will frustrate and dissuade scammers from returning, but true businesses will understand and accept the delayed action. By refusing immediate action, you pull back the curtain of ambiguity to unveil the true nature of the offer.

Pro tip: Avoid immediate action when someone shows up at your door to sell a product or service. It will frustrate scammers and give you a chance to verify the legitimacy of the business.

Scammers will protest your delayed action, either by threatening to remove the discount from the service price or by emphasizing the imminent problem you'll face if the service isn't performed immediately. Don't give in. The extra price you'd pay for a legitimate service later is worth far more than the discount you'd receive by paying a scammer for work that is never performed or poorly executed. Time is your friend. The more time you take to make a careful decision, the more likely that decision will be a good one.

Many shoppers thoroughly investigate every feature of a new smartphone before purchase: Does it have the right memory capacity and a long battery life? Does the camera have high resolution? Does the phone have positive reviews from others? While these are excellent questions to ask before making a purchase, many buyers don't perform the same investigation on people who show up at their doors to offer work or sell a product.

How do you know if you're going to receive what you pay for without doing your homework? The simple answer is, you don't. Without conducting research on a company before agreeing to a purchase, you're at great risk of being scammed.

When someone shows up at your door with a tempting offer, don't agree to it. You can either tell that person "no" or say you'd like to think about the offer and ask for their contact information. The person may protest and try to force you into making an immediate decision, so you must be resilient and avoid giving in to their demands. If they become rude or insulting, say "I'm not interested," and close the door.

If at any time you feel physically threatened by a door-to-door salesperson, say whatever you must to close the door. Tell them that you agree to the service and need to get the money from your wallet, purse, or somewhere in the kitchen. Once you've made the scammer feel they are about to get paid, close and lock the door. Call the police immediately and tell them you feel threatened by someone at your door. Do not open the door again until the police arrive.

Never allow a door-to-door salesperson into your home. That person could either cause you harm behind closed doors or look around your home for anything valuable to steal later when it's dark outside.

If you've determined that the door-to-door salesperson is offering a service you want and they agree to delay the service and give you their contact information, do your homework. Check the company's Better Business Bureau status at bbb.org. Type the company's name into a search engine to see what others say about it. Check with any neighbors the representative claimed to have done business with and ask for their opinions on the company's performance. If a business claims to be licensed, verify that claim. Obtain the company's license number, type "check contractor license" followed by your state into a web browser, and select the official license site for your state. Type the company's license number into the website and see what turns up. Also, be sure to ask other businesses for quotes on the same task to see if the offered price is reasonable, and go with the offer that makes you feel most comfortable.

Many businesses will ask for a partial payment before beginning a service. A partial upfront payment is standard practice and acceptable, but full upfront payment is not. A reasonable upfront payment should consist of no more than 10-50 percent of the total project cost, depending on the service performed and the time it takes to complete the service. If a business insists on full payment before starting the job, find another company to provide the service.

Protect your financial well-being and physical safety by remaining skeptical when dealing with door-to-door salespeople. Always do your homework and never act immediately on any offer.

CHAPTER 16

INTERNET DATING SCAMS

Eva straightened her golden hair in front of the mirror one final time before logging on to Heart4Life, her online dating site of choice. Though she would be communicating with Francisco through instant messaging and he wouldn't be able to see her, she felt better about the encounter if she looked her best.

When the moment she'd been waiting for all day finally arrived, the butterflies in her stomach threatened to overwhelm her ability to type.

"Hello, Eva? Are you there?" Francisco typed.

Eva inhaled a calming breath before responding. "I'm here. It's good to hear from you."

"You too, my love. I'm not sure my heart could have waited another moment longer to connect with you."

Eva blushed. "Me too. I missed you."

"I almost didn't make it online. I was hit by a drunk driver last night and spent three hours in the hospital."

Eva gasped. "Oh no! Are you okay?"

"I think so. The doctors said I had a mild concussion, but I'll be all right with some rest."

"I'm so sorry. I wish I was there to help." Eva typed a frown emoticon.

"I wish you were here too, sweetie. Maybe there's another way you can help."

"Anything for you," Eva typed.

"The hospital is charging me $11,000 for the time I was there. Since the driver who hit me sped away, I can't get him to pay for it. I don't have health insurance, so I tried to negotiate with the hospital to lower the bill, but they want full payment in the next 30 days or they'll start the collection process."

"That's terrible!" Eva gasped.

"I know," Francisco replied. "I can't get that much money by the end of the month, and if the late payment goes on my credit report, I might be fired from my job in security."

"Maybe you can take out a loan," Eva suggested.

"That's what I wanted to ask you. I know we haven't been together long, but if you could loan me the money, I can pay you back over time."

Eva hesitated. She had a moderate savings account that she regularly added to for retirement and could afford the loan, but the unexpected request created a flash of concern.

"I understand if you say no. You're the love of my life, and I wouldn't want you to do anything that makes you feel uncomfortable. I just want you to know that whatever you decide, it won't change how I feel about you. I still love you, and I want to marry you someday. Money will never tear us apart."

Eva had been married once before, but the man she thought she'd spend her life with died in a car accident ten years ago. Since Francisco came into her life two weeks ago, his loving words stirred feelings she thought she'd never feel again.

"It's okay. I'm happy to help. After all, if we do get married, we must be able to trust each other. I trust you, Francisco, and I love you with all my heart. Tell me what I need to do."

For the next two weeks after Eva wired Francisco the money, she tried contacting him numerous times, but he never answered her emails, and his Heart4Life account had been deleted. Her burgeoning love quickly transformed into painful humiliation. She had fallen for someone who only wanted her money, and the deep wound he inflicted turned into a permanent scar, preventing her from taking a chance on love for many years thereafter.

YOUR FINANCIALLY NEEDY INTERNET LOVE INTEREST ISN'T AFTER YOUR HEART

Thousands of people fall victim to internet dating scammers each year. It's a terrible thing to be scammed by someone who claims to be in love with you, but the reality is that scammers are everywhere, including online dating sites.

Internet dating sites are a valuable resource for finding

companionship, but it's important to keep a level head when searching for that special someone. The primary goal of an internet dating scammer is to obtain your money. If someone you've recently met on a dating site professes their love and then asks for financial help with an emergency, it's highly likely they are a scam artist. Don't send them any money, no matter how hard they tug at your heartstrings or make you feel guilty for hesitating.

You have several tools to help verify the claims of the person you're dating online. Start by typing their name into a search engine. This is the easiest step and can yield an abundance of information. If the person has social media accounts, a blog, or other internet presence, they should be easy to find. If you can't find them in a general web search, that isn't necessarily alarming, but someone using a dating site is likely to have a digital presence elsewhere.

The second step is to search the superior court website for the county they reside in. If you have their city and state of residence, type that information into a search engine followed by the word "county." Then type the county name followed by "superior court." Not every county will have a searchable database, but many do. For those that do, if the individual has been to a county court for a civil or criminal complaint, that information will be listed.

If the person has conducted transactions filed at the county recorder's office, search the county recorder database. Access a search engine, type the county they reside in followed by "county recorder," and see what turns up.

If the profile information of the person you're dating online is fake or stolen, only one or two search results will occur. They may not turn up in any database search, in which case, proceed with caution or consider other individuals on the site. The alternative is they turn up, but the information you discover is inconsistent with what they've provided, including their profile photo.

You can run their profile photo through Google's search engine to see if it has been used elsewhere. Go to images.google.com, click the camera icon on the search bar, and follow the instructions. If the results indicate the photo belongs to someone else, consider moving on to another individual on the site.

Internet dating can be rewarding as well as dangerous. If you take reasonable precautions to protect yourself and never send money to a digital date under any circumstances, you'll stand a far greater chance at a beneficial experience that doesn't break the bank.

CHAPTER 17

SHOP SMART

Janet dabbed her mouth gingerly with a white satin napkin and placed it on her empty plate. "That was delicious. Thank you."

Justin beamed. "I'm glad you liked it. I wanted to make a good impression on our first date. Did it work?" He smiled playfully.

Janet clasped her hands on the white tablecloth and leaned forward. "It did." She leaned back in the cherry wood-framed chair. "You know, you didn't have to take me to one of the most expensive restaurants in town to impress me."

Justin shrugged. "After the wonderful time I've had with you tonight, the cost was definitely worth it. You're an amazing woman, and I wouldn't change a thing."

"Will there be anything else? Dessert perhaps?" the waitress asked.

The couple, engrossed in lively conversation, hadn't noticed Jenna's arrival. Justin looked up at the bright, warm smile that matched the waitress's black pants, white long-sleeved shirt, and black vest. He turned to Janet and raised a questioning eyebrow.

Janet shook her head. "No, thank you. I think I've had enough for this year, and maybe even next."

Jenna nodded. "I'll just leave this with you then." She placed a black receipt holder vertically on the edge of the table. "Take your time."

"Hold on," Justin said. He extracted a brown leather wallet from his navy-blue blazer and fished out a credit card adorned with a local sports team logo. He tucked it into the holder. "Here you go."

Jenna retrieved the receipt holder, placed it into a hidden slot in her uniform, and gave a slight bow. "Very good, sir. I'll return shortly." She scooped up the empty dishes from the table and moved toward the kitchen.

When the waitress was out of earshot, Justin gazed into Janet's brown eyes. "To be honest, I was hoping you'd order dessert. I don't want this night to end."

Janet blushed. "It's okay. There will be others."

Justin's eyebrows perked up with hopeful enthusiasm. "So, you'll go out with me again?"

Janet glanced across the room as a waiter delivered a flaming Bananas Foster to a nearby table. "Maybe. You set a pretty high bar by bringing me here." She returned her gaze to Justin. "I can't wait to see what you have planned for next time."

"I consider it a privilege to make every encounter special." Justin reached across the table and gently took Janet's hand.

"Here you are," Jenna said as she returned to the table. She set the folder on the tablecloth and clasped her hands in front of her. "Thank you so much for dining with us tonight. Have a wonderful evening."

Justin nodded at Jenna. "The service was excellent. Thank you."

Jenna smiled and departed.

Reluctantly, Justin released Janet's hand and retrieved his card and the receipts from the folder. He tucked the card into his wallet and wrote a few figures on one of the receipts before placing it back in the folder. "Shall we?" he asked, slipping a copy of the receipt into his blazer pocket. Justin stood and extended his hand to Janet.

Janet stood and took his offered hand. "Let's."

Jenna watched as Justin and Janet exited the restaurant hand in hand. She smiled at the pleasant sight and extracted her smartphone from her pants pocket. She entered the code to unlock the screen and flipped through a series of credit card photos, the final one displaying a sports team logo prominently.

SHOP SMART

Whenever someone uses any type of financial account to

make a payment, there is always the risk that a thief will gain access to that account. As in the scene above, someone could take a photo of credit card information when the owner isn't looking and use it for illegal purposes. Even when the card owner retains full control of their card and never hands it to anyone, another person standing too close in line at a store might have ulterior motives. That individual could use a hidden capture device to illegally record someone else's card data and raid the account later.

Aside from using cash everywhere you shop, there are steps you can take to minimize the damage a thief can do to your financial health.

To start, use a credit card when shopping, not a debit card. Credit cards usually offer zero liability in the event your account is compromised, no matter how much a thief charges. In the story above, Jenna stole Justin's credit card information. When she used that card to make purchases later, Justin wasn't liable for the charges. His bank simply deactivated the card and issued him a new one.

If Justin had used a debit card, however, Jenna would have had direct access to the cash in his checking account. She might have been able to take most or all the cash in it before he spotted the theft. When Justin finally discovered the problem, he would have to shut down the account to prevent further illegal access and open a new account. He wouldn't have access to the money Jenna stole until his bank investigated the situation and returned it. He would also have to update all his auto-pay accounts, such as utility payments, rent, car payment, and gym membership, to redirect those payments to the new checking account. Beyond these hassles, he might also be liable for a small portion of the loss.

Avoid using a debit card for purchases whenever possible to minimize your financial risk while shopping.

When you do use a credit card for purchases, be sure to pay off the balance every month. Don't let interest charges increase the cost of the items you buy. You may also receive rewards as a bonus from your card provider simply by using the card for your transactions.

Many credit card companies offer cash back and other

bonuses for using their cards. If you use a credit card to make purchases and pay off the balance every month, you not only protect the money in your checking account from thieves, but you also receive a financial reward from the credit card company for those purchases. Be sure to review the different offers available from a variety of credit card companies. Don't just pick the first one you encounter or one offered by your financial institution out of loyalty. Banks are in the business of making money, not friends. Don't feel bad about signing up for the best deal available, even if it isn't with your bank. Websites like bankrate.com can help you find the card that's right for you.

If a credit card in your wallet contains radio frequency identification (RFID) technology, it's possible a thief may gain access to your card data without ever touching it. RFID cards have a wave or other identifying logo imprinted on them. These cards allow customers to make a purchase by simply waving the card over a reader. It isn't necessary to swipe these cards in a machine, but a thief can swipe your card information with the right equipment. The thief must be very close to you to grab your RFID card information, as such cards have a very short access range. A person with a backpack, satchel, or other type of pack may brush that object against you to steal your data. If you have an RFID card, there is a way to prevent a cold criminal from stealing your data.

You can prevent a thief from swiping your RFID information by placing the card in a sleeve or wallet designed to block RFID signals. To find one with the features you need, open a page in your favorite web browser and type "RFID wallet" into the search bar. Once your RFID card is inside such a sleeve, no clever device designed by the thief can capture your card information.

While most businesses and government agencies accept credit cards, some do not due to the fees charged by credit card companies. These merchants prefer cash or debit cards to avoid extra costs. In such cases, carrying large amounts of cash isn't always practical, making the use of a debit card a necessary risk.

When you must use a debit card for a purchase, there are ways to reduce the damage a thief can cause if they gain illegal access to your account. A good strategy is to set up a secondary checking account at the same or another financial institution and use that account for everyday purchases.

Many banks charge various fees unless a depositor signs up for direct deposit, maintains a minimum balance, or uses the account frequently. Find a bank that charges zero fees to maintain your secondary checking account. Credit unions are a good place to start your search, but there are also other institutions offering reasonable services. Do your homework to avoid paying bank fees on your secondary account.

Once the account is set up, place enough money in it to cover your upcoming shopping expenses. Only use this account for everyday purchases when a credit card isn't available. Set up a digital link between the new account and your primary checking account on your bank's website and replenish the funds in your secondary account as needed. Look for a "link account" option or ask a representative how to do this. If your secondary account is compromised, you can easily shut it down and open a new one without impacting your primary account.

Besides using a credit card, a debit card from a secondary checking account, or cash for purchases, consider prepaid cards. These function like a cross between a credit card and a debit card and are supported by major card networks. They can be used wherever credit cards are accepted, such as grocery stores, gas stations, and online retailers. You can choose the amount of money to load onto the card and reload it when the balance runs low.

Prepaid cards generally offer similar protections against theft as credit cards, but they come with some drawbacks. Most prepaid cards charge an upfront fee to purchase and load the card, and additional fees to reload it later. Some cards also charge fees to withdraw cash, maintain the card monthly, or even for inactivity and balance inquiries.

An alternative to prepaid cards is purchasing a gift card. Gift cards are more limited in purchasing power, usually restricted to a single merchant, and do not offer the same protection against theft as prepaid cards. If a gift card is lost or stolen, any remaining balance may be gone forever. However, gift cards cost nothing beyond the money placed on them, and there are no transaction or monthly maintenance fees. Sometimes, merchants even offer rewards for using gift cards.

Before you go shopping, consider the financial instruments you take with you. Many people carry their entire collection of debit, credit, and other cards in their wallets. If someone loses their wallet or a thief steals it, every account becomes a target for attack. To reduce the damage a thief can cause, only take the cards you'll need during a trip and leave the rest at home.

When using a card for payment, avoid displaying it where others can see the information. Shield the card reader from prying eyes when entering your PIN. If the person next to you in line is a thief, hiding your card information and PIN will make it harder for them to steal your data.

Automated teller machines (ATMs) are also used by criminals to steal card data using card skimmers. Skimmers are small devices designed to record your card information as you slide it into the machine. These cleverly disguised devices are placed over or around the card slot. Before inserting your card into an ATM, check the slot to ensure another device isn't covering it. Wiggle the slot cover to see if it moves. If it does, don't use the ATM. If you see anything that looks like a tiny camera pointed at your card, don't use the ATM.

Even if an ATM doesn't have a visible skimming device, one could be hidden inside the card slot. If a thief gains access to your ATM card data and PIN, they can create a duplicate card and withdraw cash from your account. By the time you discover the theft, thousands could be lost. Without evidence of illegal access, banks may place the blame on you, as the transactions occurred with a valid PIN and card.

The best way to prevent a thief from using a duplicate ATM card is to shield the keypad with your hand when typing your PIN. A skimmer may read the card data, but your hand will prevent a camera from capturing your PIN. Without the PIN, the thief can't use a duplicate card to withdraw cash from your account.

Consider your options carefully when using cards to shop or withdraw cash. Making the right choices can prevent months or years of aggravation and keep your money where it belongs—in your possession.

CHAPTER 18

INVESTMENT SCAMS

"Apex International Investments. How may I direct your call?" a friendly male voice said into a telephone headset.

"Hi. Can I speak with Don Reese, please?"

"May I ask who's calling?" the AII receptionist inquired.

"Yes, Arthur McNulty."

"One moment, please." The receptionist typed a code into the phone to transfer the call to Don.

After a few moments, Don pressed a button on the side of his headset. "Go for Don."

"Hi, Don. It's Arthur," Arthur said timidly.

Don rolled his eyes. "Arthur, my friend. How's life treating you? Did you go on that cruise you were planning with the wife?"

"No. Not yet. That's kind of why I'm calling. We've had an unexpected hospital bill come up, and we need to pull $2,000 from the account to pay for it."

Don grabbed a yellow tennis ball from a holder on his desk and stood up. He straightened his blue-striped tie and began tossing the ball from one hand to the other while peering across the cubicle-laden room. "Arthur, I'm sorry to hear about your troubles. It happens to the best of us as we get older. In fact, just last week, I had to go in for an annual checkup. Do you know the doctor wanted to charge me extra for the exam? Sure, I expected to shell out a few bucks for the co-pay, but $300 for the extra time it took him to give me the once-over? I told the guy he could talk to my insurance provider if he wanted more. Otherwise, forget about it. Do you know what he told me?"

"Well, um, no," Arthur replied.

"He said he'd talk with the company to see what he can do. Of course, the company paid him, but it was easier and quicker to get the money from me. It just takes a little push sometimes to get what you want, you know? Just like that Kentalon Pharmaceuticals stock we picked up for you the other month. Wow, has that thing taken off. Have you seen your account statement recently? I tell you, that's some of the easiest money I've made for a client, but it's not done going up yet. I hear they have a new dermal regenerator coming onto the market soon. That'll speed the healing process of injuries. Can you believe that? I never thought I'd live to see the day. Anyway, now's a fantastic time to add to your holdings before the stock really takes off. I'm talking four times your money here in the next six months. That's incredible! How about I put you down for another ten grand before that happens? You'll have an extra forty thousand in your account before Christmas. I bet you can take your wife on one heck of a cruise then, right?"

"Probably, but I don't have $10,000 right now. I just need—"

"I understand times are a little tough," Don interrupted. He set the tennis ball back onto his desk and peered at a glass trophy next to it with the words "Apex International Investments – Salesman of the Year" etched into its marble base. "Believe me, I know, but if I didn't let you add to your portfolio before the stock takes off, I'd feel horrible a few months from now when you asked me why I didn't insist you buy more. I don't want you to be mad at me later for passing up this opportunity now, so how about I put you down for $5,000? I would think that 20 grand in your pocket by the end of the year would sure come in handy to pay for medical bills, and you'd still have enough left over for a pretty sweet cruise. How soon can you send the money?"

"I... I might be able to use my emergency fund to pay the hospital bill. I'd only have $2,000 left though. I can't invest another $5,000."

Don flashed a wide smile. "I think $2,000 will get you a nice gain by the end of the year, Arthur. I don't know how long I can get you in at this price though, since the company could make an announcement any day now. Tell you what. If you promise to express the check to me today, I'll have my assistant place the order now to lock you in. I'll even cut my commission in half to make sure you can buy as many shares as possible. How does that sound?"

"I guess that's okay. Thank you. I appreciate your help."

"Hey, what are friends for, right? Hold on, and I'll transfer you to Jill so she can place the order. I look forward to those vacation photos you and Alice are going to send me when you get back from your cruise."

"Thank you. I think we'll try going to..."

Don abruptly ended the conversation, tapping a key combination on his phone to transfer the call to Jill. "That's how you do it right there, people," he announced loudly to the room, "another easy two grand. Top that, Johnson." He pumped his fists triumphantly into the air.

A man in his 20s wearing a red tie and white shirt in the cubicle next to Don snorted. "Yeah, yeah. We'll see who's on top by the end of the week. It's still only Wednesday."

INVESTMENT SCAMS

There are many types of investment scams, with new ones cropping up all the time. While determining whether an investment is fraudulent can be difficult, there are certain characteristics they typically employ:

Time-sensitive offers: Scammers want you to act before you think. One of the best ways to convince someone to invest money with a stranger is to push the immediate expiration of the offer. If you don't buy now, you'll miss out on an incredible opportunity to make a lot of money and regret it for the rest of your life.

High returns: People aren't as likely to invest with a stranger for a low return. The carrot of gain isn't as large as the stick of potential pain if the financial professional turns out to be a bad adviser. However, if the scammer makes the carrot large enough to be irresistible, even some of the most conservative investors will pause to consider the offer.

Communal success: When someone accomplishes a task successfully, others who see that success may attempt to replicate it. This is particularly true in investing. Scammers may tell a target that others have already made a lot of money on this or similar investments, and that the potential investor can still get on board before the investment really takes off. The scammer may also mention the name of a well-known investor who has invested with them to give the investment credibility.

Edge of success: Scammers may tell you that a company is about to announce a new product release, and once it does, the stock will skyrocket in value. They claim that if you invest in the company before that happens, your investment will increase several times over. Even if this were true, trading stocks based on insider information is illegal. A scammer may also try to persuade you to buy into a company before it goes public (begins trading on the stock exchange). While companies do go public every year, why would a stranger call you to share in the gains?

Guaranteed success: There is no investment that can pair high reward and zero risk. All investments come with risks. Even municipal bonds issued by city governments aren't guaranteed, as some cities have filed for bankruptcy and forced bondholders to accept less than their initial investments. If a city can't guarantee a return on an investment, it's unlikely a stranger offering an investment with a high return can do it.

No license: Stock brokers and investment advisers must be licensed to sell securities. Scammers aren't interested in obtaining such a license—they just want to steal your money. If you ask someone attempting to sell an investment if they are licensed, someone who is licensed will tell you. If the person makes excuses why a license isn't required, that person might be a scammer. You can check to see if someone is licensed by going to FINRA's BrokerCheck.

Scammers will peddle their wares through flashy advertising in the mail, impressive-looking websites, and well-spoken telephone advisers. They will use all means to contact new targets for their scams. Sooner or later, you're likely to receive an email, postcard, or other sales pitch from these unscrupulous people. Don't let them score a payday by stealing your money.

Look for the warning signs listed above—they might give you an indication the offer is a scam. When in doubt, throw away the advertising, delete the email, or hang up the phone. Your future financial well-being depends on it.

CHAPTER 19

CHARITABLE DONATIONS

Julia opened her old but still functional clamshell flip phone and pressed it to her ear. "Hello?"

"Hi, Julia?"

"Yes."

"It's Rick from the Hurricane Bauer Relief Fund. How are you today?"

"Oh, I'm fine."

"That's good to hear. Hey, I'm just calling to thank you again for the donation you sent last week. We've been able to buy food and clothing for a lot of people, thanks to your generosity."

"You're welcome," Julia beamed. "I'm glad I could help."

"I was hoping you'd say that. As you know, we're still receiving a lot of people in our camp who lost their homes to the hurricane. It's creating more of a strain on our resources than we thought it would, and we sure could use your help again."

Julia hesitated. "Well, I don't know. I've already sent all I could spare this month, and I haven't been grocery shopping yet."

"I understand, Julia, and believe me, I wouldn't be asking if the need wasn't so great." Rick paused. "I had to do one of the hardest things I've ever done in my career a few minutes ago. Do you know what that was?"

"No," Julia replied.

"I had to turn away two families because I didn't have the resources to help them. I felt absolutely awful, Julia, because I know that if I just had a few dollars more, I could have provided them with shelter and food. The kids looked so hungry, and I couldn't help them. Please, if there's anything you can spare, we would be eternally grateful."

Julia closed her eyes. "How much did you need?"

"Another $500 would allow me to rent another trailer and buy enough food to take care of the two families I turned away."

"Oh, I can't do that."

"Is there anything you could sell to get the money?" Rick persisted. "I can still catch the families before they walk too far. Please, they have nowhere to go and nothing to eat tonight. I don't know how much longer they'll make it out there without your support."

Julia looked around her living room at a 20-year-old television, inexpensive figurines on glass shelves, and furniture that was clean but outdated. Then she remembered her husband's stamp collection.

"Well, I have my husband's stamp collection. He used to enjoy gazing at them for hours once a month, and he always looked forward to adding to the collection when the Post Office released a new set. It was his pride and joy."

"That might be enough," Rick encouraged. "Do you think you could take it to a local pawn shop and see what they'll pay for them?"

Julia felt a pang of sorrow at the thought of selling her husband's prized stamp collection. She skimmed through the thick, leather-bound book from time to time, running her hand across its textured surface as though touching it would in some way connect her with Alex. Julia always returned the book to where he last placed it before his death.

"If it will help keep the families safe, I guess I really don't have a choice."

"You're doing the right thing, Julia. I'm proud of you, and I'll bet your husband would be too. I'll text you the address of a pawn shop near you. Take the collection there and wire the money to me the same way you did last time. While you're doing that, I'll pick up the families and bring them back to the camp. I'll also contact the rental company and have them deliver another trailer. I can't thank you enough for your generosity, and I'm sure the families you helped rescue today would say the same."

When the call ended, Rick turned to his partner in crime. "I got her for another $500. How did you do?"

"Only $50. The tightwad has a rent payment to make and

can't afford more than that right now."

"Ha! Loser," Rick chided. "You should have pressed him to sell something for the money. It worked for me."

"Yeah, yeah. Guess who's buying the beer tonight?"

Rick shrugged. "After milking this lady for an easy grand in the past week, I can afford it."

AVOID DONATING MONEY TO A SCAMMER

Scammers use a lot of tricks to convince people to send money, including impersonating a charity. These scoundrels will take advantage of people who are willing and eager to help others. The only cause that scammers support is their own greed.

Should you avoid giving money to charities that call you on the phone, show up at your door, or send you an email to prevent the possibility of getting scammed? Not at all. If you want to donate money to a charity, do it, but make sure it's a legitimate charity and that the person you're speaking with is actually from the organization before you give them anything.

Before sending money to any organization, even if you've already donated as in the story above, verify from an independent source that what a person has told you is accurate. A good way to do that is to type the name of the organization into an internet search engine and see what surfaces. Add the word "scam" to the search to pinpoint any troubles that other donors may have had with the company. You can also check the Better Business Bureau at BBB.gov to see if there are any complaints against the company and charitynavigator.org to obtain detailed data on the charity.

Even if the company checks out as a legitimate non-profit, it doesn't mean that the person who contacted you is from the organization. To verify this, obtain the name of the individual on the phone or at your door, and if you're interested in donating to the cause, ask the person to call or return later. If they claim that isn't possible and insist you donate while they are still there, say you're not interested and hang up the phone or close the door. It's likely the individual is a scammer.

If the person agrees to call or return later, the next step is to verify their identity. Type the name of the organization into your internet search engine and go to the company's website to obtain its contact information if you don't already have it from your previous search. Call the company and ask if the individual who contacted you is a representative. If not, warn the company about the person.

Pro Tip: Err on the side of caution when dealing with representatives of non-profit entities to avoid donating your hard-earned dollars to an unscrupulous scammer. Verify both the legitimacy of the charity and the representative before you consider donating.

After you've verified the legitimacy of the charity and the representative, use only a check or credit card to make the donation. It provides a traceable means to track the flow of money back to the organization if the need arises, and ensures you can verify to the IRS that you've made the contribution when you file your taxes.

Scammers will tug at your heartstrings to convince you to donate money to a worthy cause. Always make sure you're donating your money to the right cause before sending anyone a single dime.

CHAPTER 20

FRIENDS AND FAMILY

Fred checked his watch for the fourth time in ten minutes. "Betty, come on. The concert starts in less than an hour."

"Just a minute," Betty replied, as she continued digging through her jewelry box. Despite searching several times, she couldn't find what she was looking for.

Fred looked over Betty's shoulder and peered into the box. "Wear the pearl earrings. They match your blouse."

"Really, Fred? White pearls with a white top?" She stared in dismay at his black suit jacket, white dress shirt, and a hideous green and orange striped tie. "I guess I shouldn't be surprised at your suggestion considering that tie. Come here."

Betty removed Fred's tie and fetched a black one from the closet. She wrapped it around his neck and skillfully tied a crisp knot. "There. That's how you're supposed to look at the theater."

Fred rolled his eyes. "Are we ready now?"

"I still don't know what happened to my ruby earrings. They were here a month ago, after the Johnsons' holiday party and then poof." Betty made a 'poof' gesture with her hands. "They didn't just get up and walk away."

"We can look for them later, but if we want to get to the show in time, we have to go, unless you want to stay in and watch the game?" Fred looked at Betty with hopeful eyes.

Betty poked at Fred's slightly protruding belly. "Not a chance, Mister."

Fred lifted his belt an inch higher to cover his recent overindulgence in fine cuisine.

"I'll just wear my sapphire ones," Betty sighed. "I don't know what's happening. That's the second pair of earrings I've lost in the past month, on top of my missing ring and platinum necklace. Do you think someone is stealing them?"

Fred placed a reassuring hand on Betty's shoulder. "We'll search the house from top to bottom this weekend. I'm sure they'll turn up."

Betty nodded. "You're probably right."

As the couple left the bedroom and moved into the living room, their 24-year-old daughter, Stephanie, whistled. "Wow, don't you two look nice!"

Fred smoothed his tie. "Thanks. I picked it out myself." He winked at Betty.

Betty shook her head and opened the front door. "Come on, Sinatra. We have a date with Mozart."

"We'll be home late tonight, so don't wait up," Fred said.

"Have fun, Dad."

Fred nodded at Stephanie and closed the door behind him.

Stephanie peered through the front window and waved at her parents as they drove away. When they were out of sight, she moved into their bedroom and rummaged through the open jewelry box. "Dammit, she took the blue ones," Stephanie grumbled. "I could have pawned them for an easy hundred." She searched through the box until she found an onyx ring surrounded by diamonds. "Ooh, this should get an easy $250." Stephanie pulled her cell phone from her pocket and pressed a pre-programmed number from her contacts list.

"Yeah?" a gruff voice answered.

"Don't close early tonight," Stephanie said. "I've got something you're going to want to see."

THE PEOPLE CLOSEST TO YOU CAN SOMETIMES HURT YOU THE MOST

Scammers and thieves aren't always strangers—sometimes the people closest to you can find themselves in situations that make them desperate for money. Desperation might drive them to take your assets to improve their circumstances. When family members or friends resort to stealing from you to fix their problems, they're likely to continue doing so to keep fixing their future problems.

Some people develop habits such as gambling, drug use, or even shopping, which require considerable amounts of money to sustain. Once they run out of their own funds, they look for other sources of cash. They'll sell their assets to pawn shops, ask family and friends for loans, and cut back on essentials. When these sources are insufficient, they may resort to other means to fuel their addictions.

Someone looking for their next fix may lie to you when asking for money, manufacturing problems you can't ignore. The problem could be a child needing food, a car that requires repair, or utilities that need to be turned back on. Scammers will tug at your heartstrings, leaving you with little choice but to help them.

It's difficult to need help, and even more difficult to ask for it. If a family member or friend needs assistance, it might be within your power to provide aid and pull that person out of a tough situation. Doing so has dual benefits—it improves the life of the one you love and makes you feel good for having rendered aid. However, if that person continues to ask for help regularly, should you eventually say no? How can you tell if the person is using the money for the reasons they claimed?

The first question is a personal choice only you can make. The second question, however, can be addressed through certain measures. While it may not always be possible to ensure others are using the money for the stated purposes, there are steps you can take to make sure the money is spent as intended.

Instead of handing over cash or writing a check to a loved one, offer to pay for the item or expense directly. If the person needs food for a child, take them shopping. If a car needs repair, go to the repair shop and pay the bill. If utilities need to be turned back on, go with the person to pay the bill. By paying directly, you know the money is being used for the intended purpose. If the loved one insists on getting cash to handle the matter alone, they may not be using the money as stated.

You're the one with the resources, and you set the rules for how that help is given. If a loved one who consistently asks for money insists on cash or a cash equivalent, you might decide to refuse their request. This can be hard when the person is standing in front of you, but it's up to you to decide. You risk enabling a habit that could harm the loved one or their children.

If you say no, the person may yell, call you names, or question your love for them. When people resort to such behavior, it's likely because they want to use your money for something you wouldn't approve of.

Keep in mind that a person facing addiction isn't the same person you used to know. The addiction controls their actions, and they will do what it takes to satisfy their habit. Love others, but don't let loved ones destroy you. If someone becomes violent and causes you physical harm, call the authorities and report the incident. It's the only way to prevent further harm.

Sometimes, instead of directly confronting you, a loved one who wants money will resort to other means to get what they need. They might steal electronics, jewelry, and other valuable items to sell at a pawn shop, as in the example at the beginning of this chapter. A loved one might steal your debit card, checks, or take cash from a safe or strongbox in your house. If you confront the person you suspect of theft, they are likely to deny it and may become irate that you don't trust them.

When thieves are confronted with a crime they've committed, they often choose to attack in order to defend themselves. They'll launch a brutal verbal assault to shut down your accusation and prevent further questioning. They do this because it works—don't fall for it.

If you know someone has stolen from you, there are three options to prevent it from happening again. The first is to call the authorities and report the crime. However, unless the thief confesses or you have direct evidence, they are likely to deny the charges and avoid prosecution. The second option is to ban the person from your house. Denying access makes it significantly more difficult for them to steal from you. Refusing to take action means the person will probably steal again. Without consequences, criminals are likely to continue their crimes. Either option is likely to damage or destroy your relationship with the person, so think carefully before making a decision.

"What if the person lives with me, and I can't expel him from my house?"

That's where the third option comes into play. If someone you suspect of stealing lives in your home and you are unable or unwilling to alter that arrangement, you can take steps to protect your valuables.

Secure Valuables in a Biometric Safe: Place small, high-value items in a secure location only you can access. Typically, this means purchasing a safe, but not just any safe—find one with a biometric component, such as fingerprint identification. A biometric safe is more secure than a combination or key-based unit, as a thief can't gain access without your fingerprint. While a fingerprint safe defeats amateur thieves, some have override keys. To enhance security, store the key in a location the potential thief cannot access.

Manage Safe Keys Effectively: Even if you carry the safe keys with you when you leave home, consider where to store them when you're asleep or in the shower. Lock the keys in a secure location at work, leave them with a trusted friend, or give them to your lawyer. This ensures the suspect cannot access them.

Install a Heavy, Professionally Anchored Safe: To prevent the thief from taking the safe to a professional for cracking, buy a large, heavy safe, and have it professionally installed. Installers can anchor it to make removal extremely difficult for an amateur.

Use Magnetic Door Alarms: To know when someone is entering or exiting your home while you're in another room, install magnetic door alarms. They are inexpensive, battery-operated, and easy to install. These alarms emit a loud sound when the door opens, alerting you to any movement.

Set Up Indoor Surveillance Cameras: Surveillance cameras can help identify and catch thieves. For around $150, you can purchase a two-camera system with night vision, Wi-Fi connectivity, motion sensors, two-way audio, and great clarity. These units show what's happening in your home and record activity for later viewing. Some systems can also send you an email if they detect motion while you're away.

Use Webcam Surveillance Software: If you're on a budget, use a computer with a webcam and surveillance software. Many options provide similar features to more expensive systems, including motion detection and email alerts. Ensure the video is recorded to a location other than the camera itself to prevent losing evidence if the thief takes the camera.

Position Cameras Strategically: Position the camera to capture the exit point the thief is likely to use. Add a password to your computer to prevent the suspect from modifying software settings or deleting data. If the camera is set to email photos, you can see who took your computer if it's missing when you return home.

Remember, only you can choose to act if a loved one turns against you. Be prepared to defend yourself against any criminal, including the ones you hold most dear to your heart.

CHAPTER 21

MONITOR YOUR CREDIT

Kate dropped the stack of mail she retrieved from her mailbox onto the dining table. She flipped through advertisements, requests for donations, and bills until she spotted an official-looking envelope from a law firm. Kate squinted at the unexpected discovery.

"Chris, is there something you need to tell me?" Kate called out.

Chris paused in the middle of washing dishes, his eyes wide in surprise. "Look, let me explain. It's not what you think. I get these cravings from time to time, and to make them go away, I just pop one in my mouth. It makes everything feel better, at least for a while. I know the doctor said I need to eliminate sweets from my diet, but I swear I don't do it often."

Kate peered through the archway into the kitchen. "What are you talking about?"

"I'm not sure," Chris said hesitantly. "What are you talking about?"

"We got a letter from the Law Offices of Boyd and Fitch. Do you know what it's about?"

Chris exhaled in relief. "No, never heard of them. What do they want?"

Kate opened the letter and read the enclosed five-page document. "It's a notice to appear in court. It says we owe $7,254 in credit card principal, interest, and legal fees. Did you buy something and not tell me about it?"

Chris dried his hands with a dish towel and moved into the dining room. "Let me see that."

After reading the document, Chris stared at the paper as if it were an offending odor. "This is ridiculous. I've never even heard of this credit card company. It has to be a mistake."

"Maybe you should call the law firm and find out. I'm sure they can clear it up."

Chris shook his head. "You know how I feel about lawyers. I'm calling the credit card company itself to see what they have to say about it."

"Good idea," Kate supported. She watched as Chris picked up his cell phone and connected with the company. After a series of intense discussions with several employees, Chris finally connected with someone in the recovery department.

"As my associate told you, we have yet to receive payment on your account since you opened it last year," said the agent. "We had no choice but to pursue legal action to protect our interests."

"I never opened an account with your company," Chris insisted. "How could I owe you money?"

"If that's accurate, sir, then you need to talk to our fraud department. Hold on while I connect you."

Chris groaned and placed his hand over the phone. "They're connecting me to the fraud department."

"Do you think someone stole our identities?" Kate asked.

"I don't know. Probably. We certainly didn't buy any clothes in Texas or fishing gear in North Carolina. I've never even been to either state."

"Neither have I," Kate said. "What do we do now?"

"I'll find out."

When Chris finished his conversation with a representative in the fraud department, he set his phone on the table and sat down.

"What did they say?" Kate asked.

"They're going to stop the lawsuit while they investigate. She suggested we contact the credit bureau and put a fraud alert on our account. She also said we should check our credit report for any other unauthorized activity."

"Could there be other accounts out there we didn't open?"

Chris shrugged. "I hope not. I've never bothered to check."

Kate narrowed her gaze at the legal paperwork on the table. "Well, that's going to change from now on. We don't want to see any more of those." She pointed at the unpleasant document.

"Yeah," Chris agreed. "I just hope it's not too late."

MONITOR YOUR CREDIT

Even if you follow all the advice provided in previous sections of this book, a determined thief or skilled hacker might still find a way to compromise your financial accounts or steal your identity. The best way to find out if this is occurring is to check your credit on a regular basis.

Monitoring your credit doesn't have to be expensive to be effective. In fact, you can obtain your credit history from the big three credit bureaus for free.

Thanks to the Fair Credit Reporting Act, consumers are entitled to one free credit report from each of the big three reporting agencies every 12 months. This includes Experian, Equifax, and TransUnion. You don't have to contact the individual companies to obtain the reports—they can be ordered online at annualcreditreport.com or by calling 1-877-322-8228. Be prepared to provide your name, address, social security number, and date of birth before obtaining the information.

If you access a website or are in contact with a company that requests payment for your free credit reports, you are being scammed. Free credit reports are free, and you don't need to pay a dime to obtain them if you go to the website or call the telephone number above.

While you could obtain free credit reports from all three companies at the same time each year, it's better to stagger them to gain maximum visibility year-round. Plan to request a free credit report from one company, wait four months to request the second, and wait another four months before requesting the third. This ensures you can check your report frequently and act quickly to stop fraud, reducing the damage a thief can cause to your finances.

In addition to obtaining a free credit report to spot criminal activity, many reputable companies will monitor your credit daily and alert you to any changes in your credit file. Some offer limited versions of these services for free in exchange for the chance to pitch various credit card, mortgage loan, and other offers to you. Other companies charge a monthly or annual fee for these services. It's worth the effort and cost to sign up for these services to have that level of protection, especially if you want to know about changes to your credit file immediately so you can act fast. Each of the three major credit bureaus offers such a service, as do other companies. Be sure to comparison shop among the available options, and pick the right service for you at the price you're willing to pay.

When you obtain your credit report, look for activity such as higher balances owed on credit cards than you charged and accounts that you never opened. Either is a strong indication of fraudulent activity. Also, review your contact information, such as your address, to make sure it's accurate. An identity thief will apply for credit using something other than your real contact information. Scammers don't want you to find out what they're doing, and that means changing your contact information to something they control. Be sure to also review your credit inquiry history. If a thief is attempting to obtain credit in your name but hasn't yet received it, this is where that information will show up. Requests for credit accounts that you didn't authorize are an indication that a thief has targeted you.

If, after obtaining a credit report, you spot fraudulent activity, immediately place a fraud alert on your credit by contacting one of the following credit reporting agencies:

- Equifax: Equifax.com/creditreportassistance or 1-888-766-0008

- TransUnion: TransUnion.com/fraud or 1-800-680-7289

- Experian: Experian.com/fraudalert or 1-888-397-3742

Once you do, that company will contact the others to share the fraud alert information. Afterward, contact the company or companies where the fraud occurred and ask to speak with the fraud department. Tell the representative that someone has stolen your identity and is using your name and information to open an account. Company contact information is either listed directly on the credit report, or you can obtain it online. The representative may ask if you've filed a police report. Tell the representative that you'll call back with the police report information once you have it, and then follow up with them when you do.

Next, contact your local police department and file a report. You may need this information to show evidence of the crime to creditors. Finally, after these steps are completed, report your identity theft to the Federal Trade Commission by going to ftccomplaintassistant.gov. In addition to filing a report that will help law enforcement with its investigation, the site will also provide valuable information you can use to get through your experience and steps you can take to reduce the chances of it happening again.

The earlier you catch suspicious activity with your identity, the better your chances are at preventing a scammer from causing too much damage to your financial reputation.

CHAPTER 22

HOW TO SPOT A THIEF

Tom was about to stuff a forkful of beans into his mouth when his eyes narrowed at the television screen. "No, you idiot, don't open the door!" he yelled.

With frustrating resignation, Tom watched as a bucket of green slime fell onto the hero when he opened the door.

"Told ya so," Tom scolded. He rammed the fork into his mouth, savoring the maple-flavored beans interspersed with peppered bacon. He closed his eyes and moaned, enjoying the rich taste his doctor had warned him against.

Just before Tom managed to plow another heaping forkful of beans into his mouth, the house phone rang.

"Bah," Tom grumbled. He dropped his fork onto the large plastic plate resting on his stomach and reached across the armrest of his worn but plush easy chair to grab the cordless phone.

"Yeah?" Tom said bluntly.

"Hi, are you the man of the house?" a cheerful male voice asked.

Tom pulled the phone away from his face and stared at it curiously. After a second of consideration, he pressed it back to his ear. "What kind of fool question is that? I'm 76 years old. What do you think?"

"I'm just making sure, sir. You sound young for your age."

Tom scowled at the obvious attempt at flattery. "Okay, what are you selling?"

"Oh, nothing, sir. You see, I'm a scammer. You know about scam artists?"

Tom's jaw slackened in surprise. "I know what a scammer is. Why are you calling me?"

"That's easy. I want you to send me $500, and in return, I

won't send you a thing. I prefer wire transfers, but I'll accept cash in the mail if you insist."

"Is this a joke?"

"Not at all. I make a pretty good living scamming people, and I thought I'd give you the chance to contribute. There's a new smart watch that caught my eye at the store yesterday, and I'd like enough money from you to go pick it up."

"You've gotta be crazy," Tom said incredulously. "Why would I just give you money?"

"People do it all the time. Last week, I really scored big. I told a gullible woman near your age that she just won the European lottery. I took her for an easy ten grand to pay the taxes on her winnings. And just this morning, I told a guy he won a trip to Bermuda. All he had to do was pay the insurance and administrative fees to lock it in. Just like that, I had another $300 in my pocket. Easy money..."

Tom's mind took a moment to process the gravity of what the scammer had told him. "How can you do that to good people? Don't you have a conscience?"

"Consciences are overrated. Besides, we all have to make a living somehow."

Tom's nostrils flared in anger. "I'm calling the police and turning you in. You're not getting away with this."

"Don't bother. By the time they get involved, I'll have ditched this pay-as-you-go phone and picked up another. These throwaway phones are fantastic. So, how about it? Can I count on you for that $500?"

"Drop dead, you thief," Tom spat. "I hope you rot in hell."

"Thanks for the advice, but I've got a long, rich life to live off suckers that fall for anything. Tell you what, I'll call you again next week to see if you've changed your mind. Shall we say around 2:30 in the afternoon?"

Tom slammed his phone back into its cradle, spilling his plate of food across his red Hawaiian shirt in the process.

"I take that as a no," the scammer said to the "Call ended" screen on his phone.

HOW TO SPOT A THIEF

Most scammers are experts at disguising their identity. Unlike in the scenario above, skilled scammers won't tell you they want to steal your money, and they'll make it difficult for you to identify them as scammers. They will disguise themselves as allies, trusted partners, experts, and even friends or family. They'll tell you whatever they must and establish whatever emotional connection they can to rip you off. It's not always easy to identify a scammer, and sometimes you'll never see it coming until it's too late.

Despite the difficulty in identifying scammers, there are a few signs that the person you're dealing with could be attempting to steal from you:

- They threaten, bully, and intimidate you into giving them what they want.

- They make you feel uninformed and belittle your expertise or tell you how superior their knowledge is compared to yours.

- They make you feel smart by doing what they tell you to do, or they'll praise your decision-making ability by taking their advice.

- They pressure you to make a quick decision to prevent you from saying no.

These are common tactics used by scammers throughout time. They've been around for so long because they're effective and can be used with great success, no matter what technology exists at the time to implement them. A scammer will use these techniques to apply tremendous pressure on you and make you feel compelled to give them what they want, even if it's just so they'll go away and leave you alone. If you give these dirt bags what they want, they will never leave you alone.

Once a scammer identifies you as easy prey, they'll approach you again and again until the well has dried up, and you're left with nothing but heartache and a one-way ticket to poverty.

Even if the amount a scammer requests is small, such as $20, paying it will only make you more of a target. Think of the process as a fisherman looking for a place at a lake to spend his time. He'll bait the hook, cast out the line, and wait for a nibble. If nothing happens, he'll move elsewhere and try again until he gets a bite. Once he receives that bite, he'll stay in that area until he pulls out every fish he wants. When he's ready to move on, he might tell his buddies where he caught so many fish. Every fisherman he knows will then converge on that area and take as many fish as they can before there are no more fish to catch.

That fishing area is everything you own, and once you nibble on a scam, your contact information has a strong chance of ending up on a suckers list used by every con artist with access to it. They'll send you as many scams as they can create.

Don't get yourself labeled as a sucker. If someone calls and uses any of the tactics above to get something from you, hang up the phone. Deprive scammers of your hard-earned dollars, or they'll certainly be back for more.

CHAPTER 23

HOW TO GET RID OF A TELESCAMMER

Telephone-based scammers will say anything to convince you to agree to their scams. Aggressive telemarketers often employ similar techniques to get you to send them money. In my opinion, they are no better than the thieves this book warns you about.

Scammers and telemarketers want you to say "yes" to sending them money. When you're on the phone with someone who wants you to do something you don't want to do, can you say no?

Before a scammer picks up the phone to call their next potential victim, they prepare a plan of attack. They are likely to have prepared scripts honed from years of experience, rebuttals to get past your excuses, and years of practice in making people say "yes" to their offers. It's only fair that you have your own set of plans to stop this attack.

Keep the following action items near your phone, so you'll know what to do when a scammer calls:

SALES AND PRIZES

Here's what to do and say when you're on the phone with someone attempting to sell you something or wanting payment in exchange for a prize:

1. **Stay calm.** Don't let the aggressive tone or language used by the scammer tear down your defenses.

2. **Don't divulge personal information.** A scammer may ask probing questions to get you to reveal more about yourself. Don't fall for it. Never reveal any

information to a scammer that can and will be used against you, including your name.

3. **Say, "I'm not interested. Don't call me again."**

4. **Hang up the phone immediately.** If you wait for a response, the scammer may press you even harder to keep you on the line. The longer you're on the phone with the scammer, the greater the chance they will be able to break down your defenses.

5. **Make a note of the telephone number the scammer used to call you.** Never answer a call from this number again.

To make it easy to identify scammers who call with the same number they've used before, record the telephone numbers they use in your personal contacts list on your phone, if it has such a capability. Use the word "SCAMMER" as the name of the contact and never answer a call from that name. While not all scammers use the same number twice, some do. Adding such a label to phone numbers will help you avoid calls from lazy scammers who choose not to get a new phone number.

JAIL AND LEGAL ACTION

Here's what to do and say if a caller claims to be from a law enforcement or government agency and threatens you with a lawsuit or arrest unless you send money immediately:

1. **Stay calm.** Don't let the aggressive tone or language used by the scammer tear down your defenses.

2. **Don't divulge personal information.** A scammer may ask probing questions to get you to reveal more about yourself. Don't fall for it. Never reveal any information to a scammer that can and will be used against you, including your name.

3. Say, "I believe this is a scam. I'm going to contact your office to verify what you told me."

4. **Hang up the phone immediately.** If you wait for a response, the scammer may press you even harder to keep you on the line. The longer you're on the phone with the scammer, the greater the chance they will be able to break down your defenses.

5. **Write down the name of the caller, the law enforcement or government agency the caller said they were with, the action the caller claims you committed that warrants the payment, and the telephone number of the caller.**

6. **Access the internet and find the contact information for the law enforcement or government agency the caller claimed to be with.** Call that office and explain what happened. Provide the information you wrote down.

Law enforcement and government agencies won't call you to demand immediate payment with a wire transfer or money card, but scammers will. Don't let a telephone threat from someone claiming to be from the government make you afraid to say no.

When you're in contact with a scammer, it's up to you to prevent yourself from being scammed. Use the action items above to stop a telescammer from stealing your money.

CHAPTER 24

IF YOU'VE BEEN SCAMMED

If you feel that you may have been scammed, **do not send any more money to the scammer.** How do you know if you've already been scammed? There are two main indications that you're dealing with a scammer:

- If the person you're dealing with makes excuses for why they can't fulfill their end of the deal but continues to ask for additional money to move the deal forward, it could be a scam.

- If the person states that an ongoing project needs additional resources but can't provide evidence of any activity, it could be a scam.

When someone has already sent $100, $1,000, $10,000, or more to a scammer, they may feel too invested in the scammer's promises to withdraw. The individual could choose to continue sending as much money as the scammer requests, hoping that the scammer will eventually deliver on their promises.

Scammers will never deliver on what they promise.

Ultimately, these thieves will take all your money and leave you broke after they've drained you dry. When they've taken every liquid asset they can, they'll convince you to sell your car, mortgage your house, and sell your jewelry to send them more money. They will destroy you financially and laugh all the way to the bank. They'll brag to their friends about how much money they took from you and then look for their next victim to repeat the process.

People who steal from you don't care if they hurt you. They care about themselves and what they can buy with your money. Thieves aren't your friends. They won't feel sorry for taking all your money, and they will never send it back if you tell them how much they hurt you. Remember that the next time you answer the phone and someone wants you to send them money. Scammers will lie and tell you whatever you want to hear or whatever will scare you into giving them your money. Don't send them another dime.

What to Do If You've Been Scammed

1. **Contact the Local Police:** The first thing to do after you're convinced you've been scammed is to call the local police. Tell them what happened and give them as much detail about your interaction with the scammer as possible. Don't feel embarrassed about being scammed. It happens to many people of all ages, genders, and ethnicities each year, and you're definitely not alone. In fact, scammers are counting on your silence so they can keep stealing from people. Don't help them hurt others by remaining silent.

2. **Report to the United States Postal Inspection Service:** If you've received communication from a fraudster by mail or sent them money through the mail, call the United States Postal Inspection Service at 1-877-876-2455 or go to postalinspectors.uspis.gov and tell them what happened. Postal Inspectors may be able to recover your funds if the money is still in transit and hasn't yet fallen into the hands of the scammers. Time is of the essence, and the sooner you report the crime, the greater the chance your money can be recovered.

3. **Educate Yourself About Scams:** The third step is to

learn as much as possible about scams to avoid becoming a repeat victim. Keep this book handy, and use the tips and tools contained in it to guard against scammers' deceptive tricks. Stay current on news events to learn of any new tactics scammers are using to steal money or identities. A variety of government websites offer tips on spotting scams, such as stopfraud.gov, usa.gov, ftc.gov, fbi.gov, and postalinspectors.uspis.gov. Other non-government sites that offer awareness tips include fraud.org, stopseniorscams.org, ripoffreport.com, and of course, ownyourdefense.net.

Thieves add new tricks to their arsenal every day, and it's up to you to keep up with them to ensure you know what to look out for.

CHAPTER 25

HELPFUL WEBSITES

Thank You for Reading Scam-Free Living: How to Prevent Scammers from Stealing Your Hard-Earned Money

The world is filled with thieves who want to take your hard-earned cash from you. It's my goal to provide you with both the tools and self-assurance you need to stop these evildoers from succeeding.

This book presents many situations outlining how a crook will try to rip you off, but this is by no means a comprehensive collection of every conceivable way someone might try to steal from you. I encourage you to continue your studies by reading books from other authors, visiting the helpful collection of websites below, and subscribing to ownyourdefense.net for the latest tips to keep your money in your own pockets.

Stay safe.

Helpful Websites to Learn More About Fraud:

- OnGuard Online: Government Fraud Awareness Website: https://www.onguardonline.gov/

- Federal Trade Commission: Consumer Information: https://www.consumer.ftc.gov/scam-alerts

- Consumer Financial Protection Bureau: http://www.consumerfinance.gov/

- Federal Bureau of Investigations: Common Fraud Schemes: https://www.fbi.gov/scams-safety/fraud

- U.S. Postal Inspection Service: Scheme Alerts: https://postalinspectors.uspis.gov/pressroom/schemealerts.aspx

- Securities and Exchange Commission: Investor Alerts and Bulletins: http://www.sec.gov/investor/alerts

- USA.gov: Scams and Frauds: https://www.usa.gov/scams-and-frauds

CHAPTER 26

ABOUT OWN YOUR DEFENSE

Evil preys on the uninformed to survive. It uses many disguises to convince a target of its righteous or indispensable purpose, and it strikes swiftly to slip past a target's defenses before they can be deployed. Will you be ready when evil targets you?

Own Your Defense is a website designed to provide you with two powerful tools that will aid you in your quest to defend against a criminal's evil intent—awareness and knowledge. Awareness keeps you informed about a criminal's latest schemes. Pair that awareness with the knowledge you need to avoid becoming a scammer's next victim, and you'll stand a far greater chance of shielding your assets and identity from their evil intentions.

The title of the website tells you everything you need to know about surviving a thief's attack. Nobody will stand between you and a fraudster's manipulative scheme when it's launched against you. No law enforcement agency can guarantee you'll get your money back when scammers fool you into handing it over. Nobody can erase your personal information from the deepest underground caverns of the internet if an identity thief fools you into giving your data to them.

You are the only person capable of preventing a thief from stealing what's yours. It's up to you to learn when you're under attack by a criminal, and you must stop the attack before it's successful. You must own your defense.

You're not alone in your quest to defend yourself against fraud. Everyone is a potential target for underhanded thieves looking for easy money, and each documented attack some crook employs is a potential resource for you to learn how they implement their latest tricks and traps. The more you learn about how criminals deploy their trickery, the greater the chance you'll be able to identify their attacks when they target you—and they will find you. You will be targeted, sooner or later. Prepare yourself in advance of that attack and you'll have a greater chance at stopping it.

Study the material on ownyourdefense.net for tips on how to keep your money in your own pockets and download the free ebook Power Word NO. Also, be sure to review other fraud prevention websites regularly to learn about the latest fraudulent schemes.

Keep learning, and always remember that you are your first and best line of defense against criminal intents.

www.ingramcontent.com/pod-product-compliance
Lightning Source LLC
Chambersburg PA
CBHW050103230526
45470CB00004B/1665